BREAKING BARRIERS

BREAKING BARRIERS

Success Stories of India's
Leading Business Women

JANAKI KRISHNAN

JAICO PUBLISHING HOUSE

Ahmedabad Bangalore Bhopal Bhubaneswar Chennai
Delhi Hyderabad Kolkata Lucknow Mumbai

Published by Jaico Publishing House
A-2 Jash Chambers, 7-A Sir Phirozshah Mehta Road
Fort, Mumbai - 400 001
jaicopub@jaicobooks.com
www.jaicobooks.com

BREAKING BARRIERS
ISBN 978-81-8495-395-4

First Jaico Impression: 2012

Contents

INTRODUCTION

To write about successful women is always a pleasant experience, and when it is about successful Indian women, the pleasure is doubled. Women all over the world are successful in their own way, as with or without support, they happily juggle their roles of daughter, spouse, mother and caregiver, working both at home and outside. They bring up children, the future generation as it were, and are the essential bulwarks of family life, a role for which they are physiologically and sociologically equipped.

My definition of successful women, in the current context and for the purposes of this book, refers to a narrow spectrum of women who have made a name for themselves in the world of business and social enterprise, making their indelible mark in a milieu largely dominated by men.

Having been brought up in an environment and in a household where there was no differential treatment meted out on the basis of gender, my experience of any kind of bias against women, as such, is limited. I have also been extremely fortunate to have worked in organisations and with people in authority (read, men) who have given me more opportunities and recognition than I probably deserved. If there was any discrimination, it was mostly in my favour.

However, I realise that outside the cocoon of the protected bubble that I inhabit, many women do have to struggle against a lot of prejudices and discriminatory — often downright criminal — behaviour, right from the time they are born.

When I was approached to write this book, I jumped at the idea. In a country where child marriages are, lamentably, still practiced, honour killings are still prevalent, female fetuses are still aborted, where women are persecuted and divorced for giving birth to girls... women need all the encouragement and inspiration they can get, to get out of the mould that they are forced to conform to, often under the specious garb of upholding 'culture' and traditional 'values'.

The women who are chronicled in this book have been trailblazers and have risen to their current positions of eminence against all the odds stacked against them. And they have done it with dignity, without compromising on their integrity, keeping their hearts and minds fixed on their goals.

Being a woman, I understand very well the importance that role models play in our lives. During my adolescent years, I was inspired reading about the life of Marie Curie, the French-Polish Nobel Prize-winning scientist, who discovered radioactivity at the turn of the 20th century.

The story of Marie Curie is one of indomitable courage and the relentless pursuit of one's passion. As a student with scant monetary resources, she stayed in a cold, dark room in Paris and kept warm by covering herself with newspapers and sleeping under a table to keep out the cold. She could not afford lighting in her room and studied by the light of street lamps. She went on to become Professor of General Physics in the Faculty of Sciences at the Sorbonne, the first woman to hold this position.

While there is no age limit to being motivated and drawing inspiration, if it happens at a younger age, when our minds are still impressionable and more receptive to such emotions, it has a greater impact.

There is a peculiar dichotomy in the Indian social and cultural ethos. Ma Shakti is worshipped in the country as the universal emblem of female power, but girl children are unwanted. Goddess Lakshmi is revered as the fount of wealth, but girls are looked upon as a financial burden to the family. Saraswati is the goddess of learning, but when it comes to education, girls are given last priority.

It looks like women work fine as divinities, but are not acceptable as humans.

Women make up roughly 50 percent of the population, but they have minimal voting rights in terms of representation in the socio-economic-political fabric, to use corporate terminology. Men write the rules; women follow the rules.

We know that today, women are joining the workforce more than they ever did, and economic independence has gone a long way towards emancipating women from the stranglehold of a patriarchal culture where women are often treated as the second sex. But evidence suggests that progress in this area is rather slow.

A Hong Kong-based non-profit organisation, Community Business, carried out an interesting study in 2011, titled *Gender Diversity Benchmark for Asia*. The survey covered China, Hong Kong, India, Japan, Malaysia and Singapore. It interviewed women from a select sample of companies — all global corporations operating in these countries — and examined the representation of women at junior, middle and senior levels, in these companies.

The Community Business study pointed out that India was the worst performer when it came to representation at junior, middle and senior levels in the workforce. Among all the countries surveyed, India had the lowest percentage of women in the workforce.

The findings are not surprising. To begin with, in India, women make up just about 35 percent of the total workforce in the country, according to various surveys and studies conducted. That's a fairly low number. Even Malaysia, Indonesia and Philippines fare better.

Additionally, a lot of leakage happens in the transition from junior to middle levels. Compared to an average drop of 29 percent for Asia, in India, the drop was 48 percent.

Between the junior and the middle levels is when women — usually in their late 20s and early 30s — get married, have children and drop out of the career race to devote more time to their families, which accounts for the leakage. All the women whom I interviewed had supportive families — either their parents or their husbands — who allowed them to work through, without having to take a break, when their children were born.

So the scanty representation of women at senior level positions in the corporate sector is then explained by the leakage which takes place at the lower levels. The available pool of women at the middle level is already small and so the number of women who move to the senior positions is lower still.

Earlier this year *The Times of India* gave out interesting statistics from a survey done by global recruitment firm, Kelly Services. In India, when it comes to employment, the Information Technology (IT) sector is perceived as the most gender-agnostic and women-friendly sector. In keeping with this perception, there were 81 percent of women employed at junior levels in the IT sector in 2011. At the middle management levels, this value had tapered off to 16 percent, while at the senior management level, women occupied a minuscule 3 percent of the positions.

The survey explained that most women opted to quit their jobs to take care of their children and for other family reasons, and a large portion of those who quit were unable to find suitable job opportunities after the career break, despite being eminently qualified and having a good performance record.

During my interviews with the women entrepreneurs, one startling fact which stood out was that many of them were expected to get married as soon as they turned 18 years of age. Of course, the women in this book exercised their choice not to do that, choosing instead to pursue their dreams, and their parents were sensible enough to allow them. But for the vast majority of girls, do they have the luxury of that choice? Are they allowed to choose between marriage and a career?

Normally, a girl child is brought up on the notion that her main aim in life is to get married and have a family — that is her defining destiny. A career for a woman is still seen as a secondary objective. Ishita Swarup, when growing up, was subliminally given the message that she could have a career, but it would always be secondary to that of her husband's.

Jessie Paul was nearly married off at 18, and she had to persuade her family to send her to engineering college, and then further, to pursue a management degree. Suman Sahai, the strong-minded genetics scientist, was also similarly faced with the spectre of marriage when she reached adulthood.

In fact, marriage is traditionally seen as the obvious next step if the girl is not inclined towards further education. There are no other choices. Most often, marriage is the only alternative.

At this point, let me make it clear that the debate here is not about an early or late marriage, not even about marriage versus career. The debate is about choice — is a girl allowed the same choices that her male counterparts have? Are they treated on par irrespective of what they choose? Is there a level playing field for girls and boys, when it comes to taking decisions about their future?

To return to an earlier theme, in my conversations with various women, I came across some interesting insights as to why we do not see more women at senior level positions. A lot of it has to do with the male-centric attitude in companies.

Jessie Paul attributes it partly to the patriarchal culture of our society. Men feel protective towards women and do not like to send them out on project assignments. "The feeling is, we should not send this lady abroad because she has a small child. It's meant to be for the good of the woman, but of course, next year when the promotion appraisal comes up, this lady will not be considered for promotion because she has no project experience."

There are instances of over-protective fathers interfering in their daughters' careers. Kiran Mazumdar-Shaw recalls a father of one of her women employees asking her not to send his daughter on out-of-town assignments. On hearing about it, the daughter told Kiran not to pay any attention to her father as she was willing to travel for work.

Then there are other factors at play. At the top levels in an organisation — I'm talking of private sector companies here — promotions and decisions regarding who is to occupy a particular slot are made, not through the formal corporate appraisal system, but outside the office through individual rapport-building and networking, which usually happens either over golf on the weekends or over drinks in the evenings.

Women working in the corporate sector in India are still new to the culture of dropping into a bar for a few quick drinks with male colleagues or just fraternizing with senior colleagues (most of whom will be male, of course) with a view to influencing the promotion outcomes.

Since men obviously outnumber women at the workplace, there are more 'male-bonding' sessions going on all the time, from which women are excluded — partly because men feel restricted in the presence of women and also because women themselves are not too comfortable in such situations.

Regardless of how emancipated an Indian woman may be, this kind of fraternizing is not something which comes naturally to her. In many cases, the woman will have to attend to other responsibilities at home such as spending time with children or cooking dinner, so naturally she would not have the time for the 'networking' or the discussions that go on at these evening soirees.

It is also not something which is socially and culturally approved of in India and many women do not want to risk having their 'reputations' tarnished or becoming the subject of salacious gossip, and they avoid these sessions.

So the woman employee loses out primarily because she is not among the top-of-mind recall of those who are in a position to take these decisions. Of course, one can always come up with the argument that there is nothing that stops women from imitating their male colleagues and there are plenty of women who willingly and cheerfully do it but again, my point here is why must women have to follow the norms and practices set by men? Again, it boils down to the question of choice.

Besides, in the current set-up, senior male executives, who are usually the key decision-makers in companies, often do not appreciate the kind of pressures that junior women executives are working under, because most of them have wives who are not earning a living or are probably engaged in activities that allow them to manage their 'work-life balance'.

Suman spent a good part of her life in Germany, working in a laboratory environment, and she recounts having a sense of being considered not on par with men. It was not exactly discrimination nor was it an openly stated bias nor was it outright hostility, but it was tacitly understood that men had more opportunities than women, that women always had to work harder and perform at a consistently high standard. "We could not afford to slip up. If we did, we would probably have got no second chances."

A vast majority of women feel guilty over not paying enough attention to their children and families. Also, the responsibility of looking after the elderly in the family usually falls to the women. It is taken for granted that it is the women of the household who have to look after the entire family and that, of course, stems from established customs from olden times when men were traditionally the providers and women the care-givers.

Most women do not take on bigger job responsibilities that come with moving up the corporate ladder because of their commitment to their families. This happens even if they have a support structure in place, due to their innate belief that they alone can do justice to the role of family caretaker, so to speak.

A very senior executive in a state-owned insurance company recently told me that women colleagues often passed up promotions to senior management levels (which usually came with transfers), as they did not want to disrupt their family life, by a) relocating and b) devoting more time to work due to additional responsibilities that the promotion would entail.

According to him, these women who were otherwise brilliant at their work, held their own careers and jobs in lower estimation compared to those of their husbands. "They think it is their duty (to prioritise the family and home over their careers) and their husbands, families, children also feel that these women are not making any great sacrifice in forgoing their chances of moving up in their careers."

The question that begs to be answered here is — is the woman's decision governed by what is expected of her from the society she lives in or does it stem from her own inclinations? But what about the fact that her inclinations themselves are the product of societal influences, in the first place?

Vandana Luthra is a classic example — she waited eight years, till her children were older, before she started on her venture.

Women have internalised the notion that womanhood is bound to the care of others, especially husband and children. They have colluded in their own oppression by insisting on their right to manage the home and their duty in working for their family.

Suman Sahai hit the nail on the head when she said, "Women need to break out of their identities solely and exclusively as members of a family. They must understand they have an individual identity as well. And it's their legitimate right to try and manage both — it's entirely possible, with or without the support of their family."

Years of conditioning are the reason why such few women make it to the top echelons of the corporate sector. "We are all victims of our years of conditioning," said Renuka Ramnath. "That is why you feel that somebody has obliged you by giving you a career or that somebody has trusted you to let you come home late."

In general, the feeling women have is a sense of obligation rather than a sense of right when it comes to a career and a job. As Anu Aga puts it, "We feel grateful."

I would add that women are also apologetic about their 'femininity' which is seen as a sign of weakness or something to be deplored. Women, who are in positions of power, tend to emulate their male counterparts, because they think that is how it should be. Why should they?

In this connection, I was reading an article in the *Wall Street Journal* by Rupa Subramanya. The Journal had hosted an event in Mumbai, in June this year, to debate the question whether women were exercising a 'free choice' when they dropped out of the workforce or whether they were doing it under pressure in a work environment that was not sympathetic to their unique needs.

ICICI Bank boss Chanda Kochhar — herself a poster girl of a successful career woman who's reached the top — was one of the speakers at the meet.

Subramanya wrote, "Ms. Kochhar seems to believe that a woman's attitude is key in determining how far she'll rise up the ranks of the Indian corporate world. She's suggested bluntly that women who want to succeed will need to park their womanhood at the door as they enter the workplace."

With all due respect to Kochhar and her achievements, I find this statement alarming. Why should we deprecate our womanhood as something to be hidden out of sight?

Men and women are totally different in their approach to problems and that's perfectly acceptable, there's no dispute there. There is no evidence to indicate that this difference adversely impacts the end results or work efficiency or profitability of a company. Women, by nature, tend to be more empathetic and I do not see any reason why this trait should be suppressed or toned down.

Just because men have been in positions of power for years doesn't automatically give sanction to a particular method of control or management as the best. Nor does it mean that the established practice needs changing entirely. It is just one method of dealing with situations.

I think women need to get rid of this belief that to succeed in the corporate world, they need to behave like men. There is no compulsion to be 'one of the boys'. There is no shame or stigma attached to behaving like a woman — or as their instincts tell them to. Let them simply exercise their choice to be individuals.

I would now like to change direction slightly since the whole debate about representation of women at the workplace, in organisations, politics, public life, their earning potential, their ambitions, their behaviour — everything is linked inextricably to their status in the community and society, and to the treatment that this community and society metes out to them.

Women are victims of their own insecurities and lack of confidence in their abilities. Girls and women also tend to follow the path of least resistance when it comes to making a choice regarding career, marriage or anything else for that matter. The choices are made for them, and probably in the mistaken belief that they are acting in the interests of community harmony if they conform to the norms around them, they succumb to the pressures that are imposed on them, often without even realizing what is happening to them.

The insecurities and lack of confidence have their roots in the early days of childhood when girls find that they are not treated in the same way as their brothers are. With few exceptions, they are not encouraged to excel as much as the boys, either in studies or in any other area.

Even when girls are told that their destiny is to get married and have children, it is conveyed in a manner calculated to instill a sense of inferiority in their minds. A lot of importance is attached to working and earning money compared to marrying and raising kids. This attitude in the upbringing itself puts women at an emotional and mental disadvantage with respect to their purpose in life.

So pursuing a domestic life is seen as unproductive. From this stems the woman's aspiration to go out to work, earn money and be 'productive'. I find this rather perplexing. Why can't a woman who looks after the household and brings up healthy, intelligent children be treated on par with a woman or man who goes out and earns money?

To illustrate this, I would like to quote a conversation between a doctor and a male farm worker, sourced from an International Labour Organisation document of 1977:

"Have you many children?" the doctor asked.

"God has not been good to me. Of fifteen born, only nine live," he (the man) answered.

"Does your wife work?"

"No, she stays at home."

"I see. How does she spend her day?"

"Well, she gets up at four in the morning, fetches water and wood, makes the fire and cooks breakfast. Then she goes to the river and washes clothes. After that, she goes to town to get corn ground and buys what we need in the market. Then she cooks the mid-day meal."

"You come home at mid-day?"

"No, no, she brings the meal to me in the fields — about 3 kilometres from home."

"And after that?"

"Well, she takes care of the hens and pigs and of course, she looks after the children all day... Then she prepares the supper so it is ready when I come home."

"Does she go to bed after supper?"

"No, I do. She has things to do around the house, until about nine o' clock."

"But, of course, you say your wife doesn't work?"

"Of course, she doesn't work. I told you she stays at home."

An earning woman is automatically accorded more respect than a non-earning woman. Housework, looking after the needs of the family, and domestic duties are not seen as 'work' in the real sense of the term. That is why we have the peculiar terminology of 'working' and 'non-working' women.

Of course, this is an old argument and one can go on pontificating on the injustice and ill-logic of this all-pervading belief.

The question I'm trying to raise here is not whether women should or should not have a career; whether women should or should not marry; whether a woman should pay more attention to her home or career. The question is of choice. A woman should have the choice to decide what she wants to pursue. The choice should not be made for her or forced upon her as an obligation or as a duty — or because it has been made acceptable by tradition and convention. And she should not have to be made to feel guilty over whatever she chooses.

Women, by their whole attitude and language, are subservient to the whims of their men folk.

When a man says he has a supportive wife, he probably means that she takes care of the entire domestic front, of the complete family including the children and older relatives, totally absolving him of all family responsibilities and leaving him free to pay undivided attention to his work. On the flip-side, when a woman says she has a supportive husband, she probably means that he is 'allowing' her to work outside the home and earn money. However, this woman will probably find herself attending to domestic chores as well.

I have many friends who tell me, 'I'm very lucky, my husband and in-laws do not have any problem with my working.'

This statement, in itself, is an admission that women are constantly seeking approval and permission to do things which are seen as outside the scope of their natural duties and obligations.

Why should the husband have any objection to a woman earning money in the first place? Why should the woman feel that she has to have that sanction before she takes up a job that earns money?

Tradition has created a social hierarchy on the basis of sexual division of labour whereby men are at the top and women at the bottom. However, anthropology and history suggest that while this division of labour has been prevalent throughout human history, it was not always a hierarchical one. This means that its origin is much more recent (relatively speaking) and can be reversed, with sufficient effort.

There are studies to show that the sexual division of labour has led to such hierarchical culture, with men taking upon themselves the mantle of the superior race. From being the provider to being the oppressor, is but a short step. So if we want to dismantle the hierarchical structure, we have to eradicate division of labour on the basis of sex — that is, we need to stop considering certain occupations or vocations as more suitable than others for women.

I do not consider myself a rabid feminist consumed by a burning desire for equality with men — indeed I do not see that (equality with men) as any benchmark to which I or any woman should want to aspire to. The minute we ask for equality, we arrogate an inferior status to ourselves and we have to change that mentality.

What I want to stress upon here is that parents should ensure that their girls are given every opportunity to realise their potential — especially in terms of learning and education in whatever field they choose, and they should have the choice to exercise their rights — their rights as a human being and as an individual.

Men should not appropriate the responsibility of deciding what a woman should do or how she should conduct herself. We cannot be used as symbols of oppression and depredation, when different communities of men want to assert their authority over each other. That is what we are fighting against — that men should not assert their supremacy or their superiority by subjugating women or committing atrocities against them.

I would like to place on record a couple of points here about this book. The book is not just about chronicling the lives of the women who feature here. Many of them are well known and have been written about extensively and I'm sure, for many of those who closely follow corporate developments in India, much of it would be familiar ground.

I also do not want to create an impression that all men are responsible for the current suppressed representation of women in industry. There are plenty of men who are doing their best to support and encourage women in their endeavours to go forward. As I said earlier, I have received only support and encouragement from all the men I have been privileged to work with.

While the achievements of the women in their chosen careers are at the core of the stories in this book, I have tried to provide some insights into their minds and their early lives to bring out the fact that most of them had to face gender prejudices and challenges along the way. These women became successful because they challenged these attitudes and refused to accept the status quo — to the extent of defying parental diktats.

The stories are illustrations to try and tell you that anything is possible, provided you have a sense of purpose and believe in yourself. The women in these stories started out as ordinary girls, they had their own demons and insecurities to battle with and ultimately, they triumphed, to become extraordinary women.

I hope this book inspires millions of girls and women out there to shake off their lethargy, unshackle their minds from generations of ingrained subservience to antiquated oppressive attitudes, and to live their lives as individuals with a sense of purpose.

All of us are extraordinary with lots of talents — we just need to work towards bringing out this hidden potential. Circumstances may be against us but then we owe it to ourselves to fight to change our situations.

As Suman Sahai said, "Remember, you hold up half the sky. It wouldn't happen without you."

ASK AND YOU SHALL RECEIVE

Jessie Paul

Founder and CEO
Paul Writer Strategic Services

Nazareth is a tiny village in Thoothukudi district in Tamil Nadu, located about 80 km north-east from Kanyakumari on the southern tip of India. It's so small, it's not likely to show up on a map. Predominantly a Christian town, its most prominent feature is a more-than-a-century-old church.

It was here in the winter of 1982 that 11-year-old Jessie found herself, transported from a school for gifted children in Sydney, Australia and faced with the task of learning Tamil, her mother tongue and yet an alien language.

She had six months in which to learn it. She took it in her

stride, a characteristic which was to define her attitude to occurrences later in life: the death of her father at a crucial juncture, refusing marriage at an early age and opting for further education, joining an engineering college in Trichy against her parents' wishes, leaving a well-paying job with a big corporate house to pursue a management degree — all decisions which eventually led her to fulfilling her dreams of working with some of the best companies in India, achieving her ambitions and finally striking out on her own.

Jessie Paul, founder of Paul Writer, a B2B company which provides marketing advisory services to companies and hosts conferences for marketing chiefs, is the quintessential small-town girl who made it big. In India, if you are a girl born in a small town, if you belong to a middle-class family whose only bread winner is ailing, if your family's finances are not too good and then you get a proposal for marriage from a reasonably well-off family — nobody would be surprised if you settled for marriage as a way out of all your troubles; if you were an ordinary girl, that is.

But Jessie was not an ordinary girl. Even if she was not consumed with a burning ambition to be 'someone', she had enough drive not to be just 'anyone'.

But, we are getting ahead of ourselves. Let's rewind a bit.

Jessie's father was in the foreign services and liable to be posted anywhere, within India or overseas. She had just begun schooling in Delhi when her father was transferred to Sydney, Australia. After four years there, it was back to India, leaving behind her two, older, college-going siblings, a brother and a sister, to complete their education.

Jessie and her parents settled in their native Nazareth. She was admitted to one of Nazareth's oldest schools, the same one in which her mother had studied.

Jessie was a consistent topper in her class. In her whimsical words, "In Nazareth, you tended to be an over-achiever because you were told that otherwise you would end up as a teacher in Nazareth. This alone was very big motivation to study like crazy. Nazareth produced toppers because everybody was desperate to get out of the place."

Being ranked 12th in the state in the 10th standard board exams and getting 'decent' marks in the 12th, got her the 'ticket' to get out of the place.

As in the case of most children, the values that were to stand her in good stead in her adult years, were imbibed from her parents. From her father she learnt that if she wanted something, she should go ask for it. You couldn't expect others — especially your parents — to do the asking for you. From her mother she learnt adaptability — the ability to adjust to all situations and become comfortable in whichever sphere she found herself.

When Jessie turned 18, she received her first marriage proposal. Her schooling finished, the parents of the prospective groom approached her family. It was a difficult period for Jessie and her parents. Her father was undergoing dialysis and the family's finances were getting drained, the money going towards his treatment and her education.

The 'boy' was well-settled and her family "were not unwilling," to see her married. But Jessie turned down the proposal and her parents agreed. This was the first of the three, what can be called, 'inflection points' in Jessie's life.

She admits, "Not getting married at 18, that was the first big resistance really." In India, the pressure (to get married) comes not only from parents but also from extended family members who exert their moral authority in such matters.

That and persuading her parents to send her to engineering school. "That was a bit of a struggle."

The Programmer Who Found her Passion in Marketing

At that time, law, medicine and engineering were popular career choices for most middle-class Indian families. A retired High Court judge told Jessie that the legal profession was an acceptable choice only if she knew someone sufficiently influential in that field to get a decent clerkship, without which it would be difficult to make an advantageous start. Young, resident doctors also advised her against entering the medical field. So that left engineering.

Her brother was a computer engineer, and since she had some exposure to computers, Jessie opted to study Computer Science, vaguely harbouring ideas of becoming a computer programmer. She was weak at Maths but her brother assured her that that would not pose a problem for her in pursuing the course.

She had set her heart on joining the Regional Engineering College (REC) in Trichy, while her parents wanted her to study in Madurai, which was closer home. She got admitted to Madurai, but within a short time got a call from Trichy, where she had been waitlisted.

She had no time to inform her parents. A friend managed to get her to an aunt's place in Trichy, while a male cousin escorted her to the college.

At the college, Jessie told the principal, "I'll join you, if I can study Computer Science."

The principal, rather struck by this imperious request and probably even more struck by the girl who had come all alone and did not need the guidance of her parents to make her choice, conceded to it.

At REC Trichy, Jessie learnt a vital lesson — not to persist with something you are only mediocre at.

"We had one or two geniuses in college. There was one programming genius in particular, who did not have to put in any effort and would still arrive at the most elegant code. Most of us would have struggled with the coding, probably copied it from some other guy and we would have 25 lines of code at the end of it. He (the resident genius) would then stroll in with three lines of code which produced the same result."

"So you knew that you were never going to be really good, not even if you tried really hard, because that required a different type of thinking. So by then, I knew that I wasn't going to be this hot-shot programmer. I simply didn't have it."

On graduating from REC Trichy, she joined the technology design firm, Tata Elxsi. At the time, the company used to supply and set up computer work stations for Tata Group firms and state-owned undertakings in India. It was also a loss-making company.

"We had no idea about anything. Tata's was a big name, the salary was good," says Jessie. Her batch was the first to join the company as women engineers. "They had only had women secretaries working there till then."

If you ask Jessie what she did during her stint with Tata Elxsi, she says, with a giggle, "Preparing for CAT." CAT is Common Admission Test, the entrance exam to get admission to the coveted Indian Institutes of Management.

Jessie was a trainer as part of the sales support team in Tata Elxsi. One year into the job, she found that she was not having 'much fun'. By that time, Jessie had discovered her flair for marketing and event management having become friends with a girl who was in the marketing department. Jessie worked with her on a couple of assignments and they also did an event together in Mumbai. "This seemed like something I would enjoy."

Hence IIM. This was the second inflection point for Jessie — leaving a well-paying job, with an established company belonging to the illustrious Tata Group, for further education and an uncertain future.

She had to use all her persuasive skills to convince her mother, who was now single after her husband had passed away in 1990, to part-fund her management course. The argument was that it would be worthwhile leaving the current job to study for a management degree, which would get her a better and higher-paying job later.

"It could have been a bad decision, but in retrospect, it turned out to be good," says Jessie.

Her mother sold off their house to pay for her daughter's IIM fees.

At Tata Elxsi, while she was training a client in Dewas, in Madhya Pradesh, on December 6, 1992, riots broke out in nearby Ayodhya in Uttar Pradesh, following the demolition of the Babri Masjid mosque.

The CAT exams were postponed due to the riots and this gave her the time to better prepare for the exam. She cleared and got admission to the Indian Institute of Management in Joka (near Kolkata).

Lessons in Advertising and Marketing

Jessie studied Marketing Management at IIM, Calcutta between 1993 and 1995. It was here that she met her future husband, whom she married in 1996, a year after she graduated from the institute.

Jessie also became aware of a compelling skill that she possessed, which she would leverage in her future career — the ability to make comprehensive project presentations. Her growing expertise in making presentations made her a sought-after team member.

"If you have good presentation skills you can get away with a lot of other stuff," is Jessie's summation of her skill.

In 1995, she joined advertising firm Ogilvy & Mather as an account manager, at a salary which was just on par with what she had been earning when she was with Tata Elxsi — a move which flummoxed her mother.

"There were expectations," says Jessie. After all, her mother had sold off the only asset they had, the family's ancestral house, to finance her daughter's studies, all on the assumption that the degree would be the ticket to riches ahead.

But Jessie was resolute. She wanted a career in marketing and advertising and O&M was her entry point to that world. O&M did not come to the campus for recruitments. The other companies which did, did not make her an offer, finding her over-qualified for the jobs they had. Stubbornly, Jessie decided that if O&M would not come to her, she would go to O&M.

So that's what she did and got what she wanted. The mantra 'If you want something, you should go and ask for it' was paying off.

At Ogilvy & Mather, Jessie started off servicing some of the regional tea brands of Hindustan Unilever, the Indian unit of the Anglo-Dutch multinational Unilever.

Some of the people she met during this time proved to be useful contacts, whom she could leverage when she set out on her own, years later.

"They've all gone on to become fancy CEOs now," says Jessie.

There was Shivakumar, currently Nokia's business head in Middle East, Africa and India. Then there were Ashok Venkatramani, who is currently the Chief Executive of Star News and Kanwaljit Singh, who is the Co-Founder and Head of venture capital firm, Helion Venture Partners.

All of them were willing to guide this young IIM graduate, especially Shivakumar, himself an IIM Calcutta alumnus.

Hindustan Unilever was a benevolent and mentoring client. Jessie was sent to remote and rural areas to learn about the demand for the company's products and the kind of channels they employed to push sales.

O&M too was one of those rare agencies which were not ruled by the dictum — 'The client is always right'.

When Jessie was treated rudely by a client during one of her pitches, O&M sided with her and while retaining her to service the client, they made it painless for her by cutting out her personal interactions with it.

"O&M had certain fabulous values. The client must respect you. They actually encouraged you to walk away from a client that spoke disparagingly of the agency."

The iconic firm which David Ogilvy had founded lived by certain rules and practised what it preached. They had certain expectations of a client, and the client needed to live up to those standards. Jessie has imported some of these values into her own dealings with clients, as an entrepreneur.

A prospective client who falls short, in her estimation, of being hospitable, would never make the cut. These could be simple things like not sending a car to the airport, not offering coffee, too much of nit-picking over small expenses.

"Clients who don't offer you hospitality are bad clients. It means they do not consider you a partner in the process but see you as a (cheap) vendor. In such cases, the engagement is sure not to work out."

Jessie's reasoning is that if a prospective client is unable to organise itself for its consultant, then it cannot organise itself for its own clients either.

After marriage, in 1996, Jessie had moved to Chennai with her Bengali husband, but a couple of years later, both of them wanted to return to Bangalore.

Her husband, who was with Citibank, wangled a transfer to the newly opened Citi office in Bangalore. He was earning more than she did — Jessie would compete with him on the basis of his House Rent Allowance; her entire salary was equal to his HRA compensation — and both felt the move would be beneficial.

The Indian software sector, powered by a huge workforce of English-speaking graduate engineers, was just taking off as US and European corporations were looking to outsource process-driven jobs to low-cost destinations like India. The world was getting ready to step into the 21st century, Y2K (Year 2000) was around the corner, and the country was already reaping the benefits of liberalisation, set in motion by P. V. Narasimha Rao and Manmohan Singh in 1991.

Jessie thought that it was an opportune time to monetise her engineering background. "I dusted off my engineering degree and thought that all these new IT firms would fall for the story that a Computer Science engineer plus MBA — would be a great fit for a marketing job."

Both Infosys Technologies and Wipro made offers; the latter offering her a position with Wipro Infotech (the personal computers division) and the former in general marketing.

What clinched the outcome in favour of Infosys was its offer of stock options. Her father-in-law advised her — "Have you seen the Infosys shares recently? If they are offering you stock options, I think you should take it." Jessie still has those Infosys shares in her possession.

Infosys: The Globe-Trotting Global Brand Manager

Jessie joined Infosys in 1998. She says founder Narayana Murthy gave her the job, owing partly to her knowledge of English and partly to her presentation skills.

Murthy was, till then, still making corporate pitches to clients on his own — not trusting anybody else to do the job as well as he could. "Till I came along," Jessie says, tongue-in-cheek.

Infosys was then in a high-growth phase. Jessie remembers having frequent meetings and brainstorming sessions with Narayana Murthy, Nandan Nilekani and Phaneesh Murthy, who was the global head of marketing. It was an unforgettable mentoring experience. They were even available to offer career advice, Nandan also helping her with her positioning in the organisation.

"I don't think they have that kind of time now."

It has been nearly nine years since she left Infosys, but she makes it a point to meet Murthy once a year, who is still interested in what she is doing.

Jessie was Global Brand Manager and responsible for projecting Infosys as a global brand along with Marketing and Communications. She spear-headed the team that set up the marketing department in the company, establishing the necessary infrastructure and processes. She also wrote the company manuals which are in use, even today.

Her role included field marketing programmes, such as the Wharton Infosys Business Transformation Award, which she anchored, and which got Infosys the US-based IT Services Marketing Association's Diamond Award. She was also part of the team involved in the Nasdaq listing of Infosys' American Depository Shares in 1999.

It was a heady ride for Jessie. Presentations, of course, and travel, as Infosys did not have any marketing people overseas those days. She travelled all over the world, with her field events and customer forums in the US and Europe in her bid to spread the Infosys brand. "In three years flat, I saw most of the world. We had customer forums everywhere." Including Monte Carlo, with helicopter rides thrown in.

Infosys taught her to be value-conscious and to see the benefits of intelligent economising. Narayana Murthy believed in leading by example and living by his values. He did not expect anyone else to do anything which he himself would not do. He travelled Economy Class. He had no qualms about staying in budget hotels like Best Western.

"One thing I've learned from Infosys is that respect matters more than financial benefits. If you have respect, the money will come."

While her career was flying high at Infosys, there was something missing. Jessie's goal was to be the Chief Marketing Officer of a Fortune 1000 company by the age of 35 and time was running out for her. She had to do something, and fast.

In 2003, she joined start-up back-office firm Quintant Corporation, as its Global Marketing Head. Hers was one of the high profile exits from Infosys that year, after Phaneesh Murthy, who left the company following a sexual harassment case which was settled out of court. Quintant, which offered transactional pricing services, had Phaneesh Murthy for an advisor.

Again, it was one of those decisions which could have gone either way. Narayana Murthy advised her against leaving Infosys as there was still a year to go for many of her stock options to mature. But Jessie's goals were set higher than mere stock options.

Barely had she joined Quintant before it was acquired by iGate Corp — with Phaneesh Murthy as the Chief Executive. It was not what Jessie had bargained for. From an exciting new start-up firm, "we all became people in iGate, which was no fun."

Jessie's move to Quintant was dictated by her ambitions. She didn't think she was going to be Head of Marketing in Infosys for a long time. There was a lot of churn in the company after Phaneesh left and there were other people with more work experience than her, vying for the job. "I didn't want to hang around indefinitely waiting for that role to come."

Wipro and Finally... CMO!

The Quintant-iGate spell lasted two years and then she got the big break she was angling for, in 2005 — Chief Marketing Officer at No.3 outsourcer Wipro.

The job at Wipro did not come by fluke. Jessie worked towards it, putting in place the connections even while she was at Infosys. She networked and made the necessary contacts with the right people — including incumbent Sangita Singh of Wipro (whom she succeeded) so that when the software company was looking for a marketing head, Jessie was the top contender for the position, with Sangita recommending her name to then Wipro CEO, Vivek Paul.

And she got the job.

"I truly believe that's the way you get a job; not by sending resumes. I have never got a job sending a resume randomly and I've always done door-to-door calling, right from my Ogilvy days."

Jessie was following her old mantra — If you want a job, you have to go ask for it. "If you send in your resume and wait for them to call you, nobody will. Or they will call you for jobs they want to give you."

She also believes that if she had followed the regular channels in landing the job at Wipro, she would never have been paid the salary that was offered her.

"Most people in India don't network with a plan to get anything."

Compared to Infosys, Wipro was a much more engineering delivery-led organisation. It was also a price negotiator, in comparison with Infosys which was a value negotiator.

As Head of Marketing in Wipro, leading a team of 50, Jessie was able to put into practice all that she had learnt about leadership as a management student. She raised the representation of women in the marketing department from just 12 percent when she joined, to 50 when she quit. She made sure that people did not work late and took her responsibilities with respect to women very seriously.

Wipro was also acquiring companies overseas and she was involved in the global integrations that the acquisitions entailed.

It was also at this point of time that she thought of starting a family. The idea came to her that now that she had achieved one of her professional goals, this would also be the right time to have a baby.

However, things do not always go as planned.

On the professional front, Jessie had raised her target bar higher. She wanted to be a CEO by the age of 40 but she lacked that crucial experience of operations and delivery, necessary for becoming the CEO — not only at Wipro, but at any other software company.

"Four years in Wipro were enough to convince me that I was not going to be the CEO of this firm, or any other IT company, because everybody would ask for delivery and operations experience.

"I was successful as the Chief Marketing Officer. But there was no guarantee that I would be equally good at operations, or even delivery (of services)," said Jessie.

Unlike the consumer goods sector where marketing is king, in a software company's hierarchy, it was still not a critical function. Delivery, of the product or services, was pivotal. "It is only when an industry starts to commoditise that the marketing function starts to become important. When you are still delivering (products or services) like in an IT company, they don't need such hot shot marketers," is Jessie's explanation.

Meanwhile, her biological clock was ticking. Both natural and artificial means to conceive were not yielding results. Jessie and her husband then decided on adoption as a feasible alternative.

Once she realised that she could not be the CEO of a software company, she looked at other marketing companies for opportunities. "But there was no attractive proposition in sight."

So then the only option was to start her own firm — and this was the third inflection point for the future entrepreneur. At Wipro, she had hit a glass ceiling of sorts and any kind of vertical career progression — at least the kind that she wanted — seemed to be full of question marks.

Her aim was clear; to be the head of a company. Though she had spent virtually most of her working life in the IT sector, her own lack of operational experience precluded her from getting the top job in any company in that sector. Her experience in marketing was extensive but finding the right industry, where her skills would prove crucial, was difficult. She also hit a roadblock in terms of monetary compensation as other industries could not match up to what the technology sector was offering.

Entrepreneur, CEO and a Mother!

Paul Writer Strategic Services was born and launched in January 2010.

In identifying her area of entrepreneurship, Jessie followed the criteria set by leadership and management guru Jim Collins.

It should be something she was passionate about, was perfect at and it should be a profitable venture.

"I couldn't find one thing which met all the three criteria."

She liked and was proficient in managing and hosting conferences. Marketing was her passion. Consulting was a profitable venture.

That was how Paul Writer was conceived. Just a few days before she walked into her new office on MG Road in Bangalore, Jessie and her husband became the parents of their adopted baby girl — the formalities being completed in a record six months, since the couple did not have too many demands as to the kind of child they were adopting.

"My first client was engaged, literally, with her sitting on my lap. She was nine months old when she was adopted," says Jessie.

Prior to launching out on her own, Jessie did the necessary groundwork by creating her own brand, independent of Wipro. "When you are in an organisation, branding helps a lot. You are identified by your organisation. But when you call as an individual, then your recognition becomes a question."

She did a lot of active branding before she left Wipro, including writing a book, *No Money Marketing* published by Tata McGraw Hill.

"If you ask me, that is something all Indian entrepreneurs should learn about. They are very successful in a firm but fail to build their brand outside of that."

The consultancy part of her business provides marketing advisory services and support to companies that need it. A company with a product to launch, or a company wanting to integrate newly acquired brands, or the Chief Executive of a new company seeing a spike in marketing requirements — these are the types of clients who approach her seeking a marketing plan.

Such companies cannot cope with the marketing requirements on their own, or do not have the right skills to deal with it, or sometimes, the team is not experienced enough.

"Our basic output is writing the marketing plan for a client." Once the plan is in place, Paul Writer finds the right people and agencies, setting up the necessary ecosystem that can implement the plan and hand-hold the client for the first three months, sometimes up to a year. Usually by that time, the client is ready to run it on its own.

CSS Corp, headed by T G (Tiger) Ramesh, is one such client for whom Paul Writer is setting up the website, building a marketing plan and showing them how to use their monetary resources effectively.

"In the marketing industry, the ecosystem for implementation is very fragmented," says Jessie.

The advantage that Paul Writer brings is that it is able to acquire the necessary people at the right price point, according to the client's requirements and budget.

Among Paul Writer's clients are an architecture firm, IT companies, a construction and real estate firm and a marketing client.

Jessie says that her consulting fees have doubled since inception. The venture is also profitable — a testimony to that being that she can pay herself a market-related salary, one of the best criteria for gauging the success of a company.

On the conferences side, she manages marketing events which are sponsored by companies, such as IBM, which has been a major sponsor-partner so far. The revenues for her conferences come from the sponsors and ticket sales for the events — that is, the participants pay to attend.

Jessie's conferences are backed by research and have a specific agenda and theme. The conferences are followed up by chats and interviews which are featured in her newsletters. This creates a value-proposition and the necessary incentive for Marketing Heads to attend her conferences.

Unlike most conferences, where only the senior people are speakers on the dais, with the rest of the attendees being junior people or vendors looking for business, her conferences ensure attendance from a large number of CMOs. As an example, she cites the conference she hosted in Gurgaon (near Delhi) which attracted 110 CMOs, including the Marketing Head of Oberoi, where the event was held.

"Most of them were surprised to see their fellow CMOs in the room." This has created a unique selling point for her events.

According to Jessie, the reason why so many conferences fail is that their structure is dictated by the sponsors and all they bring together are `talking heads' with not much of a focussed theme to explore.

The conferences business is a hugely scalable model, she says, because at the end of three years, the event would sell itself. After hosting about four events, she is still exploring a suitable pricing model for it, because it is a price-sensitive segment. If the tickets are priced too high, it would fail right at the outset.

Most people expect to attend such conferences for free. But a low price would draw a lot of people who are not of the required calibre, who do not add any value to the event, thus lowering the quality of the conference.

"The pricing is based on perception and not just the cost."

"I am here not just to maximise profits, but to build a property that I can run in future years. Three years hence, the CMO conference should be on their must-attend conferences calendar."

Jessie's aim is to make Paul Writer the hub for anything in marketing. "There are very few people in India who are talking a serious marketing language." She attributes her steady flow of business to the paucity of marketing talent in India.

"In India, there is a dearth of marketing talent and many companies are not going to succeed, only because they cannot find someone with more than five years of work experience, who has some decent knowledge of B2B marketing."

Paul Writer does not actively solicit clients, it relies on Jessie's branding and marketing skills to attract clients. "In consulting, a client who approaches you is a better client than one whom you approach."

She assiduously uses social media such as Facebook, Twitter and LinkedIn as also her newsletters to engage with people and to access prospective clients.

While having a profitably running business on her hands is encouraging, Jessie is aware that being the key person in her venture is a major threat, especially on the consulting side. The entire business is heavily dependent on her and her ability to work. "What if I fall sick?" she wonders.

None of the people working with her are equipped to step in and take charge, if she is not around for any reason. Also, as Jessie explains, her clients expect to deal with her as the head of Paul Writer, rather than with her junior colleagues.

"The CEO who gives me two lakhs a month expects to see me at least once a month, even if the operations are being handled by others (in Paul Writer). The plan can be written by anybody but they need me to go and convince them that their million dollars are being well spent..."

However, there are no plans to change this state of affairs for the next year or so. "Maybe after three years, I'll look into that." The ability to scale up the consulting side of her business is limited by this one big factor.

She is also working on revamping her website and creating higher online visibility for Paul Writer.

The Social Conscience

Jessie tends to set short, five-year goals for herself. While she is contented with herself currently, she says that in another five years, her goals may change.

Her cut-throat ambition to get ahead when she was climbing the corporate ladder has given way to a more mature, calmer person who, as she says, is "on a self-actualisation process. You can only be ambitious till you get what you want. The new me is not ambitious."

Her daughter's arrival on the scene — "a life changing experience" — has also changed her priorities. She makes it a point to be home by 7 in the evening and does not work on the weekends.

She is learning to play the piano, something which has interested her right since her childhood. Always a voracious reader, she is also catching up on books.

There are plans — nebulous now — to set up a university to dedicatedly nurture marketing talent in the sector. But that would require funds. She is in no hurry however, and is toying with the idea of raising funds to grow the conferences side of her business and to have an educational series on marketing concepts.

"But all this is in year number three — I wouldn't want to approach anyone with an unproven concept. I would rather put all the necessary elements in place and then make my move," she says.

Jessie believes her positive energy and ability to inject fun into the situation while doing her job are her USPs. "Most Indian companies tend to be gloomy and serious workplaces. So if you come out laughing and happy, people like to spend more time with you."

At the moment, Jessie doesn't envisage going back to being an employee.

"I'm having too much fun," she giggles, in her trademark style.

2

THE SEEDS OF A REVOLUTION

Dr. Suman Sahai

Founder
Gene Campaign

In the late '80s, a young Indian woman in Germany was struggling with an existential dilemma — whether to pursue her current vocation or to return to India where she could put her research and learning to use.

For a genetic scientist, with a consistently brilliant academic career culminating in her acceptance as Professor of Genetics in the University of Heidelberg in Germany, it was not an easy choice to make.

Everything that she had ever wanted in life was here in Germany. She had wanted to be a scientist and she was, a successful scientist at that. She didn't want to let go of science, she didn't want to quit university, and she didn't want to give up the life of an academic in Heidelberg.

But at the same time, she knew that global changes were in the air, changes that could have important ramifications for India, most of all rural India, where she had her roots and which she identified with strongly.

The General Agreement on Trade & Tariffs (GATT) was gaining prominence right after the Uruguay Round of trade negotiations in 1986, and developed countries, led by the United States, were demanding that an international standard for plant variety protection be imposed on all member countries.

Immersed in her scientific world, the young woman vaguely realised that patenting seeds would take away the livelihood of farmers in India and might well sound their death knell.

A United Nations conference she attended in Berlin around that time played a role in crystallising her thoughts. The theme of the conference was 'Conflict Resolutions in the Stability of the World'. The speakers were focused on warfare and the threat that terrorism posed. When it was her turn to speak, the young woman said that all the bombs and guns in the world would not threaten its stability.

"What will threaten world stability is inequity."

She explained that patenting seeds and taking away farmers' means of sustenance would create strife and unrest. "That, I see as the most dangerous threat to stability."

She was surprised when during a break in the conference, delegates came up to her to congratulate her on her speech, telling her that she was absolutely right. She had been speaking off-the-cuff, based on a superficial understanding of the issues at stake.

The reaction of the audience convinced Suman Sahai, the young woman, that she was on to something here.

The painful decision, though, had still to be made. It was a period of torture for her. She did not want to leave the scientific world but she now wanted to return to India.

The conflict in her mind was eventually resolved when she poured out her torment to two of her friends in the academic world.

She decided that she would give up her cherished life of an academic and return to India. Once the decision was made, she was at peace with herself.

Suman Sahai returned to India and took up the cudgels on behalf of the farmers, representing rural India, under the umbrella of her organisation Gene Campaign.

For Suman, scientist and social entrepreneur, that conference was a seminal experience, the trigger that led her to return to her homeland. The thought had already germinated within, before she attended the conference, though even in her mind she was unable to articulate it.

"Where do I want to be, what am I going to do," were recurring questions that haunted her as rumblings from the external world in the form of patents, WTO, GATT intruded on her scientific ruminations.

The decision that Suman took, which shaped her future career, has to be seen in the context of her overwhelming passion for science and academic research. It was one of the most critical decisions she has had to take in a career that was solely governed by her single-minded devotion to genetics.

A Modern Upbringing within a Feudal Framework

The early life of Suman Sahai, founder of Gene Campaign, reads almost like Hindi pulp fiction. She was born in a feudal, politically-connected family in Tilhar in Uttar Pradesh — the oldest town in the present-day district of Shahjahanpur. She was the eldest of three children.

The family had lived in Tilhar for more than 600 years. The environment in which Suman grew up had all the underpinnings of a tradition-bound family.

Her grandfather, the family patriarch with whom she was very close, ruled the clan with a firm but benevolent hand.

Growing up in rural India had a big bearing on Suman's entire life. "I'm extremely connected to rural India — my roots are there. My identity is there. I may have studied and worked in universities abroad, but my defining identity is this."

"I am proud of my identity as a scientist, but always as a person rooted in rural India, within a feudal framework. I understand intuitively about rural India."

Despite the feudal set-up, her parents were progressive in their outlook and sent the children off to boarding schools. Suman studied at the Maharani Gayatri Devi School in Jaipur and St. Mary's Convent in Nainital.

It was a curious upbringing for the children — the modern world of boarding schools juxtaposed with the traditional life of their family during the holidays. The children's development and their outlook to life owed a lot to this divergent exposure to two different worlds.

Marrying the traditional and progressive outlooks also made a big difference to the children's identities.

The traditional family values notwithstanding, the women in the family were strong and assertive. These values were imbibed by Suman at a very early age. The women were not cowed down and had a keen sense of their rights.

The children were also taught that honour and duty were everything.

Her grandfather's message to her was — "Never forget who you are or where you come from." Suman and her siblings grew up with a strong sense of responsibility, not only towards themselves, but also towards others.

The sciences, especially biology, fascinated Suman, right from her early days in school. "Temperamentally, I was inclined towards the sciences."

Suman excelled in studies, a trait that has marked her throughout her academic career. She enjoyed education and being educated.

Her family members recognised her brilliance and she gives full credit to her parents and uncles for allowing her to study as she wished, for letting her choose the institutions that she went to.

When she was 18 years old, the issue of marriage came up. "My parents started looking around for a boy. But when I said I wanted to pursue my education further, they did not stand in the way."

One of her uncles told her father, "Don't get her married at 18. She's brilliant. Let her follow her head, her heart... let her do what she wants. She will do something."

Still fascinated by the biological sciences, Suman went to Lucknow University and did her Masters in Botany. It was at this time that genetics began to interest her. "When I was growing up, genetics was a happening field. It was the most divinely exciting science on the horizon."

College was a curious experience for Suman. She loved the education but on another level, she was, as she says, 'tormented'. Lucknow University was a place filled with students from feudal families, hailing from the mofusil areas of Uttar Pradesh. Despite Suman's rural antecedents, due to her boarding school background, she looked and behaved and dressed differently from the others, and stuck out in the crowd.

She remembers boys lining up to stare and comment at her in the college. "Very difficult to deal with... I couldn't handle all that. But that was also a part of growing up."

Suman was a good student. She was also wild. In college, she bunked classes and was once caught by the hostel warden, with a bunch of her friends, trying to get high on aspirin dissolved in coke.

In the first year at University, her grades slipped a bit, prompting a missive from her father who wrote, "Since you are obviously not enjoying being educated, I should probably start looking for a nice boy for you."

This, of course, spurred her to greater heights of excellence, at least so far as her studies were concerned.

After college, Suman pondered on her prospects. She wanted to work in the field of genetics but she didn't know what to do and where to go. She wrote to many places to find out about prospective institutes she could join, including some overseas.

Her primary passion was genetics and she did not want to follow the route of studying biochemistry first and then studying genetics. In India, the only place that offered a doctorate degree in genetics was Indian Agricultural Research Institute (IARI) in Pusa, near Delhi.

She applied and got an interview call. "In a wonderland kind of way, I trundled off to Pusa." IARI was then a very prestigious institute and would accept only two doctoral candidates in a year, so the seats were hotly contested and sought after.

She got through the interview and was selected. "I was told what a masterly coup it was. I had no idea... I actually blundered into it."

She also came into contact with the Head of Genetics at IARI who told her, "I had to select you because you were way above the best candidate. But if I had my way, I would not have, because women waste seats. They get married... and waste the education they have had. I would have selected a boy, had I found one close to you."

This was an awkward start to a rocky relationship, especially because he was also going to teach her.

However, even after getting through the interview, Suman was hesitant about joining IARI. She had written to and was getting acceptances from universities and colleges abroad, especially from the US. Around this time, she met Dr. M. S. Swaminathan, who resolved the issue for her.

He told her, "You can go (overseas) if you like, but if you do your PhD here, you'll learn how to do research. The reason is, you'll have the courage to do all kinds of risky research here, because you don't have to prove yourself. You will be able to do all kinds of experiments here and try different kinds of things because you already have a track record. If you go abroad, you'll have to prove yourself first. And you'll probably do safe science."

"That was the best piece of advice I got. And I decided to stay," says Suman. "And I'm extremely glad I did, because it happened exactly as he said. When you have a track record and don't have anything to prove to anybody, you can do science exactly the way you want to."

The Evolution of a Scientist

Suman spent four years in IARI and had a `blast'. The institute exceeded her expectations. The quality of research was outstanding and the training intensive.

"We got super-education. We had Nobel laureates as guest lecturers and that was an amazing experience."

The students had to work hard. She herself, as an excellent academic, was put on a high credit course which ensured that she 'had to slog her butt off'.

Her thesis was on the genetics of pulses — a subject she still holds dear to her heart, especially since India imports a large part of its protein requirements.

"It has remained a bottleneck in Indian research. Pulses are our Achilles' heel. They are difficult genetic material to work with, as their chromosomes don't open up easily, unlike rice or wheat which are easier to work with. Also, unfortunately, the attention shifted to rice and wheat because we had to fulfil the green revolution. I wish pulses had remained a focus area. But it has fallen off the radar. We're still importing a huge amount of pulses. Our high agricultural import bill is due to pulses and phosphate fertilisers."

Pusa was all about hard work — and harder partying. Suman loved (and still loves) to dance. After working hard the whole day, she would go out with a gang of friends to spend the night in a frenzy of revelry.

The Oberoi hotel was the spot they hit to dance all night and then in the early hours of the morning they would go to the terrace to grab some breakfast.

"It was a dissolute life we led." That phase of her life lasted a while.

Then she would return in the morning, wearing evening clothes, grab some sleep and then head back to the labs and classes for more work.

Her partying however did not come in the way of her studies where she got straight A's.

Once she got her doctorate Suman, who wanted some more exposure in genetics, spent some time at the All India Institute of Medical Sciences to study medical genetics and get some familiarity with the issues in that area.

She also went to Edmonton, Alberta University in Canada with the specific intention of learning electron microscopy, a very important requisite for pursuing research in genetics.

The next 12 years were spent by Suman Sahai overseas, fully absorbed in the life of a genetic scientist and involved in the highest quality research.

From Edmonton she moved to Chicago University, where she spent a couple of years working on neuro-transmitters and their role in mental illnesses — as part of her work in medical genetics.

"I went overseas because there were things I wanted to do and they were available there. At that age, it was a big dream to go out there and do the best science, and work in the best labs. I wanted to work with the best scientists."

After a couple of years, the head of her team was shifting from Chicago to the West Coast and he wanted his entire team to go with him and land long-term contracts to work there.

Suman was unable to commit herself for the long term; she was already nurturing dreams of working in Heidelberg University in Germany, which was by then emerging as the centre of genetic research in Europe.

She wrote to Heidelberg and got an acceptance immediately.

The 10 years that Suman spent in Germany were one of the most thrilling and exciting phases in her life. This was what she had been working towards throughout her academic career and it was a fulfilment of all her wildest dreams.

"This was where I established myself as a scientist. This was where I really enjoyed the fruits of my education."

Her area of research in Heidelberg was the genetics of memory, the intricacies of intelligence and the biochemistry of the brain.

The Germans had a very methodical and scientific approach to research and academics, and if one wanted to do serious research, that was the best place to be. "The Germans have a fantastic academic tradition. They take their academicians very seriously and that is the basis of their research and economy."

They followed a system wherein scientists working on a particular area of research would gather together to get funding for a project. This was also an opportunity for them to interact and share their ideas, compare notes and probably collaborate on projects, if they felt the need.

"People shared ideas and they offered suggestions. It was a thrilling period. If you really wanted to live the life of an academic, this was it. I've had the most fun in my life in that period. That was the way I had imagined science and academics to be."

In those day-long get-togethers, the researchers would have

lectures and discussions, defending their work, and at the end of the day, they also had to make sure that they came back with money, because that was what it was all about.

The discussions afterwards, during the evenings and nights, over endless mugs of beer and glasses of wine, were equally stimulating.

"Everybody there is brilliant. So you're having a thrilling kind of discussion all the time. That is the one thing I miss here — the intellectual companionship and the challenge."

Institutes and labs in Germany also followed the practice of sharing equipment, if scientists were engaged in similar work. This could even extend to collaborating and co-operating in experiments and taking the work forward.

"Big breakthroughs happen when people work together. You can progress 10 times faster that way. That is the way science should be done."

Curiously enough, even in that environment of pure science and research, Suman recalls being aware of an undertone of prejudice against women. "Medical faculties in Europe are conservative to the point of being farcical."

The prejudice was never articulated or expressed in any way but a woman scientist always had to work extra hard and keep up the hard work throughout. She could not afford to slip up, because there was always a high probability that there would not be opportunities for a second chance.

"At the higher levels, you find very few women. There is a certain sense of discrimination, although unspoken."

Suman kept an even keel. She eventually went on to become a professor and part of the faculty at the University.

The Foundations of Gene Campaign

Returning to India was not easy for Suman. For the first few months, she was in misery. She had no lab, no office to go to. She did not know what to do — other than a vague sense of doing something that could prove beneficial to the rural population of India. She wanted to be relevant and useful, but how? That idea was not yet articulated.

"I would get ready in the morning and realise I had nowhere to go. I would sink into this depression..."

She had also got married by this time and was adjusting to life full-time with her husband's family. This is a part of her life she prefers to gloss over as her subsequent work did not find any support or favour with her husband or his family.

As she adjusted to the new environment, she began to look around to see where she could fit in. Trade-related Agreement on Intellectual Property Rights (TRIPS) and the issue of patents was beginning to absorb her.

"The beginnings of Gene Campaign are in IPR."

She began talking to people about it. Mohan Prakash, the president of the student union from Banaras Hindu University, was one of the key people with whom she associated, and who helped her to lay the foundations for Gene Campaign.

Suman came from a family with political connections and she thought that participating in the political process would be a good way to get an idea about all that was happening in India.

She knew the late Mr. V. P. Singh and worked with him on his election campaign in Uttar Pradesh, in 1989. She travelled throughout the state learning and observing the living conditions of people in the hinterland and remote villages.

"Being part of the political process allowed me to travel all over, to listen and to see what was happening."

"I learned how to speak at public meetings." Under the tutelage of Mohan Prakash, everywhere she went she asked people about the most pressing problems they were facing and then raised these issues in her speeches and meetings.

"This was a valuable lesson. I learned how to identify problem areas and how not to say confrontational things."

As time passed, things began to acquire clarity. "Seed patents could not be allowed. That became the rallying point for us."

Soon, with the help of Mohan Prakash and others of a similar hue, all of whom had been followers of Jayaprakash Narayan (JP) and his program of Sampoorn Kranti (Total Revolution) in the '70s, she began creating a network to mobilise public opinion against Intellectual Property Rights and what it portended for the farmers of India.

People, largely from the media, were sceptical of her claims, especially with regard to seed patents. "The text was unintelligible to many people. But I, as a geneticist, could see what it was saying."

By then, she had started writing in newspapers about her fears and apprehensions. "I realised that just writing and meeting people was not enough. We needed a platform to reach out to people."

That platform was Gene Campaign. It was formally registered in 1993, but work under that banner had already been in progress for two years.

Suman had the power to attract people, convince them and bring them around to her way of thinking. Her family and academic background coupled with her brilliant record testified to her integrity and sincerity, as also the fact that all her arguments were based on irrefutable, hard evidence and not on theories. It was a powerful magnet.

"What I conveyed was — here I was, a scientist who understood the implications of the GATT treaty, and a person from rural India who understood the implications of what it could do to them. It was very natural for someone with my background to put it together."

People from across disciplines and fields came forward to help her at this juncture.

As a start to their campaign and to create a network of like-minded people, Mohan Prakash and his associates dug out the addresses of all the people they had known during the days of their association with JP and sent out postcards to them.

"That's how we built up the network."

The message was — the seed was threatened and the seed would go. If the seed went, Indians would follow.

"We went wherever fate decided to take us and we had very interesting journeys."

From its earliest days, Gene Campaign decided on a policy of not tapping institutions to raise funds. The campaign would be sustained by the goodwill of the people who were involved in the work, who were interested in what the campaign was advocating and with the help of those who were affected the most by her work.

"We had no money and we decided not to take any. By that time I had been in India for two years and I could see the NGO racket unfolding." She was referring to the unscrupulous practices of some Non-Governmental Organisations who amassed funds under the garb of social work, but where there was never any real developmental work getting done.

"So we pooled money from our own resources. People are generous; and if they see that you are out on a limb and not doing it for self-interest, they'll come forward with contributions." She got contributions everywhere she went, including some from the government, while some others, like the Tatas, were willing to do work for them without charging a penny.

"We must have held about 400 to 500 meetings. Not a single meeting have we paid for. People would pay for it."

The upshot of this kind of a working strategy was that the people identified with it strongly. It was always "our gene campaign." They felt like a part of the movement; they were the movement.

Working with scarce funds also led to some bizarre situations, like the time she had to travel with a prominent Member of Parliament from Andhra Pradesh to Hyderabad, posing as his spouse, as that was the only way she could get a free ticket.

Help came from unexpected quarters. A journalist from Rajasthan whom she knew arranged a meeting for Gene Campaign in the state, the local journalists' association pitched in with tea and biscuits for everyone while somebody else made arrangements for their accommodation.

"Those days we used to sit and gnash our teeth over these things and how to do it. But there was always a solution. People actually helped."

"We would not have been who we were if we had not done it our way; it would never have been 'our' gene campaign. There is a sense of involvement and people honour good intentions."

She admits that coming from a feudal but elite family background, topped with an education in some of the world's best universities, and being recognised as a brilliant scientist, she has had to do a lot of learning along the way as to how to engage with people, particularly within the Indian rural ethos.

Suman strongly credits the successes that Gene Campaign has had, especially with regard to seed patents, to Mohan Prakash and his band of student followers. They responded to the call even when there was no money, no great idea. "It was possible because of all these people; they were the reason Gene Campaign became a national movement."

The clout the campaign wielded grew with every success it enjoyed. On Genetically Modified food and the US-backed initiative to include it in the agenda of the World Trade Organisations to allow trade in it, she decided to hold a consultation and got all the political parties to attend it. They prepared a draft and got all the experts to go through it, including those who were involved in the Geneva negotiations.

"We drafted things which needed to be renegotiated. That was the first time India was given a draft to think differently."

She is still a strong votary against GM crops and the attempts by pressure groups to implement field trials in India, without proper safeguards being first put in place.

"We are trying to get the attention and focus onto GM technology, trying to show how bad deals are being done. We are also enforcing technology competence in regulatory bodies along with transparency."

At present, what is consuming Suman's attention is the much-hyped Food Security Bill, which is yet to be implemented and is attracting a lot of attention, mostly to its disadvantage, as also the subject of climate change.

"The whole issue of climate change in India is focused on energy. Nobody is looking at food security."

"The Food Security Bill is the work of an idiot," says Suman, without mincing words. According to her, it is just plain political gimmickry intended to win the next elections for the Congress, just as loan waivers and the National Rural Employment Guarantee Scheme won them the previous election.

"The Bill is only about grain distribution. We already have a PDS (Public Distribution System), an ICDS (Integrated Child Development Services scheme), a Mid-day Meal scheme, an Annapurna scheme and the Antyodaya scheme. We have five government schemes to support food distribution.

"The Bill lacks complete structure and legitimacy because it is only trying to do a different kind of distribution."

It does not address the crucial issue of production, as India is in the middle of an agrarian crisis, which can no longer be ignored. The global hunger index has placed India much below some sub-Saharan African nations, where perpetual hunger reigns.

Currently, Suman Sahai is hard at work on the Hunger Campaign — an initiative to spread awareness about the shortage of food in the country and to inform that India is in danger of tipping over, much like the Arab uprisings in 2010 and 2011.

The Arab world was the scene of a wave of revolutions that consumed countries such as Tunisia, Egypt, Libya and Yemen, forcing a change in their governments, while there was simmering unrest in places like Jordan, Iraq, Algeria, Kuwait and Morocco.

Suman attributes the Arab Spring, as the wave of protests is popularly called, to anger over lack of food. "It was not about democracy. They wanted a change in government because they thought a new government would give them food."

She has a major recommendation to make — throw out the Food Bill. It has to be reworked and its whole focus changed.

If the issue of food production cannot be addressed, "it's no use bleating about food security."

She is equally strident on the need for clean water and sanitation, because insanitary conditions lead to diarrhoea. "Even if you have access to food, if you are diarrheal all the time, you will not retain the food."

The high levels of anaemia and malnutrition in areas where food is available is due to lack of hygiene. That is another aspect of food security which has to be addressed adequately.

"I think we need to attack this bill in a much more fundamental way.

"People are abandoning their fields because agriculture is not paying. The cost of production is higher than the procurement prices. If the farmers are not going to produce food, what are you going to distribute?"

Food inflation has been rising steadily despite a good monsoon in 2011 and this is because the uncertainty in production is still there.

The apathy of the government in understanding and tackling these basic issues is the biggest challenge Suman faces. "First, we have to fight our own government — an increasingly apathetic government that has no interest in rural development."

Gene Campaign is also planning a discussion on the Food Security Bill and is planning to rope in the Opposition Parties as well as Chief Ministers of various states. The Hunger Campaign, with documentary competitions and essays, will raise the issue at the ground level and among ordinary citizens, especially students.

Gene Campaign has created an aura of authenticity and responsibility around itself, partly stemming from Suman's own roots. "We will never give out a statement unless we can stand by it. That's the training."

Policy advocacy has been a particularly strong point for the organisation and Suman intends to implement it in full force in her campaign against hunger.

"There is one thing very I'm grateful for — I never have any regrets about coming back. I'm very happy that I came back to India. Because, had I had regrets, it would have been a torture for me to work here. My own commitment was very well argued.

"I have a sense of deep contentment."

●

3

THE PATH LESS TRODDEN

Ishita Swarup

Co-founder and CEO
99labels.com

Ishita Swarup had always dreamt of doing something on her own. During her college years, she had wanted to set up kiosks selling French fries and cold coffee.

Indians may have to make do with French fries from McDonald's and cold coffee from Cafe Coffee Day, because what Ishita is now selling is branded apparel and lifestyle accessories on her three-year-old online portal, 99labels.com.

Prior to this, she built and sold a telemarketing company, Orion Dialog, which ranked among the top three back-office firms at the time.

Ishita, co-founder and CEO of online, discounted fashion and lifestyle portal, 99labels.com, was born in a large joint family in Delhi with very middle-class, traditional values and beliefs.

Her parents were fairly liberal, but as in most Indian households, she was always told that her destiny was to get married like every other girl, and that even if she was earning, her income would be secondary to that of her husband.

Fortunately for Indian entrepreneurship, Ishita did not take that to heart or even if she did, she decided that she would do something to change that thought.

Her father, who was in the power and water resources department, was posted to Bhutan when Ishita was six years old. The family spent the next six years in the scenic environs of the mountain kingdom, where Ishita developed a lasting love for the hills — and trekking.

Sundays and holidays were spent trekking the mountains, nights were spent listening to the sounds of the animals that roamed the hills. It made a lifelong impression on Ishita, who even today, often takes off to the hills to unwind, and sees trekking as a way to meditate and rejuvenate.

When she was 12, the family returned to Delhi. Being born in a large family in northern India has its advantages and disadvantages. The obvious advantage is the support system that you immediately get — both physical and emotional.

The disadvantage is that you are landed with a lot of well-meaning but interfering relatives who are always trying to marry you off at every available opportunity. The Jain community in India, to which Ishita belongs, is notorious for getting their girls wedded at a very young age — at least most of the time.

When her mother decided to take up a job as a teacher to supplement the family income, Ishita grew up overnight, fending for herself and looking after her younger siblings, a brother and a sister.

Ishita's family was a curious mix of the liberal and the conservative. She was learning Kathak at the time and her family saw no problems in her travelling to various places and performing on stage. Dancing was a profession that Ishita seriously contemplated in her earlier years.

But later in life, when she worked in a hotel, that met with disapproval from her parents. Hotels - parties - bars - late nights — that was how her parents saw it. No. Not a good profession for a decently brought-up, middle-class girl.

The same ideas were attached to being an air hostess. Without informing her family, she had applied for an air hostess's job with a Dutch airline. When the call-letter came, her family almost threw a fit.

For Ishita, the airline job was not about becoming an air hostess per se — it was more about what it represented: freedom and a chance to see the world. However, when her parents put the veto on it, she did not protest too much and gave it up because her heart was not really in it anyway.

After school, she studied Economics at Delhi University — and this was where her first foundation, to becoming a business entrepreneur, was laid.

College over, Ishita debated what to do. And it was at this time that she had a brief stint with the hotel industry.

Later, still undecided, she took up an assignment with the travel division of American Express Bank, a move which her family thoroughly approved of, since it fit their notions of a respectable job in the corporate sector.

"But I hated it, hated every second of it," says Ishita.

She was part of the back-office operations in the bank, surrounded by management graduates and 'strait-laced corporate types.' It stifled her.

She ended it within a year, thinking she would never work in a bank again.

However, this experience opened her eyes to the potential opportunities that a management degree would give her in terms of career choices. She thought maybe that was what was needed to help her achieve her goals.

What were her goals, what did she truly want? A high-flying job in the corporate sector? To travel the world? To be her own boss? Whatever it was, it was definitely not the usual path of marriage, kids and a suburban home, living out the lives that millions of other women got stuck in, either because of a lack of choice or because they opted for the easy way out and followed the line of least resistance.

Ishita took all the management entrance exams she knew of and landed in the Institute of Management Technology in Ghaziabad, suitably near Delhi for her family not to raise too much of an objection.

In India in the early '90s, a management degree in marketing was a ticket to the corporate world. Ishita, who was fascinated by people, and by the art of managing them, took on Human Resources as extra credit during her course. When chocolates and ice-cream multinational Cadbury's came scouting for fresh graduates, Ishita was one of those who got snapped up.

Cadbury's and Dollops

Ishita's first stint as an employee in the corporate sector lasted about three years. Sales, marketing, brand management — the drill that most management trainees go through. And her family was happy. Their eldest daughter had done all the right things — she was a management graduate, she had a good job with a prestigious company like Cadbury's, what more could anyone ask for? Now all that remained was for her to marry and 'settle down' — something which Ishita was steadfastly resisting.

Her quest had not ended — in fact, it had not even begun. Her mind was busy churning ideas for something to do on her own.

Her job with Cadbury's only served to convince her that she was not cut out for a corporate life — with its set rules and regulations. If she rebelled against authority at home, submitting to authority at her corporate workplace was even more irksome.

There was another element to it. "There were people around me who used to say that they wanted to be a CEO by age 40, and I used to think I'm not going to wait that long to be a CEO."

Her last assignment with Cadbury's was handling the Dollops ice-cream brand in Delhi. When Dollops was sold to Unilever, she faced the unpalatable prospect of being sent back to Mumbai again.

That decided it for her. She did not want to move out of Delhi and she quit — predictably provoking another storm in her family, who thought she was quite crazy to have chucked the perfect career.

It was one of those turning points which come into almost everyone's lives, but which many fail to act upon, instead choosing to tread the safe path of a salaried employee, as they do not want to run the risk of pursuing their passion and failing in it.

Ishita, at 27, was curiously unafraid. "When we started the company, we weren't sure what we were doing and had no fixed business plans. My parents were furious (at my leaving Cadbury's) and I told them that if in one year I couldn't support myself (in my venture) I would go back to a regular job."

Orion — The First Start-Up

It was 1994. The Indian markets were just recovering from the turmoil caused by the Harshad Mehta stock market scandal, and the newly set-up securities watchdog Securities and Exchange Board of India, under S. S. Nadkarni, was struggling to clean up and make investing safer for retail investors. The great IPO (Initial Public Offerings) boom had just started and plantation companies were out to dupe gullible investors. Mobile telephony was yet to flag off...

It was against the backdrop of this economic climate that Ishita and her friend Tina — with an initial capital of Rs 5,000 each — started off a tele-marketing firm, Orion Dialog, probably among the very first back-office firms to be launched in the country. Citibank was their first client.

Ishita cut her teeth on Orion — in its 11 years of existence, this was the company where she learnt all she did about starting a business, keeping it afloat, running it, even pulling it out of near-dissolution at one point of time, even when her Chartered Accountant advised her to simply shut the business down and cut her losses.

"I made all the mistakes that I possibly could in this time," she says. "That was my learning school."

When she started off, she had only her own courage and conviction to support her. Her family, including her parents, were totally disapproving of what they considered a foolhardy venture.

It was a battle everywhere.

The venture, the concept, was new. The two girls did not even have a proper business plan — it evolved as they went along and got clients. They worked out of a small room rented from a friend, who was running his own business in the premises.

India was still in the early days of liberalisation, and entrepreneurship, especially by women who were little more than girls, was still a novelty.

"We were young and we looked even younger," says Ishita. She and her partner were often asked by prospective clients if they could speak to their boss. Or they wanted to speak to their fathers, who, they were convinced, were backing the girls' venture.

Gender prejudices were rampant. Ishita recalls making a presentation to a senior official in a bank. At the end of the presentation, he asked, "When do you plan to get married?"

"Is that your question," she asked. "If I were a man, would you have asked the same thing?"

"Well..." said the banker. 'If you marry and move away with your husband, what happens to the company? Who will look after it?"

Ishita felt piqued by this but on reflection, realised that the question was based on reality. Women marry and more often than not, the norm is that they follow their husbands, putting their own careers and aspirations on the backburner.

The client was just voicing a concern propelled by an established fact, which he had no reason to believe would not be justified in this case.

She weathered these episodes. But funding was important and bank finances were difficult to get. Angel funding or venture funding was not a common concept in those days. "We grew through internal accruals." During the initial months, they had very little overheads, so whatever they made was a profit. "All the profit was channelled back into the business." The lack of funds taught them to economise and make efficient use of available resources.

And Ishita, who had a poor head for finance, made plenty of mistakes. As she says now, she learnt economising and bootstrap budgeting from her Orion days.

"Even now, I don't like finance but I understand the importance of running a tight ship. However large the revenues you make, if you don't have control over your costs, you are never going to make profits."

A couple of years after she started Orion, she ran into trouble. Deep trouble. The company was expanding and they needed to set up new offices and hire more people. Suddenly, costs started to go up, and "we made some bad decisions."

The girls were told to close down their venture — it was going nowhere.

But Ishita was not going to give up. She persevered — she knew there was a demand for the kind of services they were offering; she knew that if they could ride this out, they would achieve the success they were looking for.

"I knew something they did not; I could see something they did not."

That vision, the ability to see ahead, was key; the gamble paid off. Orion turned around. By 2005, Orion was among the top 3 BPO (Business Process Outsourcing) outfits in the country employing 2,000 people, with revenues of Rs 25 crores, servicing several large clients across the country. It was also attracting a lot of attention from industry players.

But she was again running into problems — this time from her partner. Tina's priorities were changing. She was cutting down on the time she devoted to the venture as she wanted to spend more time with her family, especially her children.

Ishita was frustrated, though she did empathise with her partner's compulsions and motives. She tried to persuade her friend, pointing out that they had weathered the worst of the lows and that now they were at a stage where they could scale up exponentially. But Tina had made up her mind.

At the same time, Orion was growing bigger and needed funds.

At this difficult juncture, Ishita decided she would get a strategic partner who would not only infuse fresh funds but also help her in the running of the venture.

Enter Aegis Logistics, the back-office outfit belonging to the Mumbai-based Essar group, run by the Ruia brothers whose business spans refineries, shipping, steel and telecom.

Aegis had been set up with the intention of catering to the telecom sector but at the time, the company was still in a fledgling stage and looking to scale up, through both organic and inorganic routes. Aparup Sengupta was the Chief Executive of the company.

Ishita approached Aegis with the intention of offering them

a stake in her company and the access to much required funds. Aegis saw this as the perfect opportunity and offered to buy her out. She accepted the deal — almost overnight.

Apart from the fact that her partner was easing herself out of the venture, Ishita herself was losing the motivation to keep Orion running. The thrill of overcoming challenges while building an enterprise was no longer there.

Orion had attained a critical size — there was no chance of it collapsing at this stage, it could only grow bigger. Ishita felt she was no longer learning anything new from it. "I had learned a lot in 11 years. There was only going to be more of the same, only on a larger scale. So I was losing interest."

She always had the option of appointing someone else to run the company, while she herself moved on to something else.

However she made her choice — selling out to Essar and making a clean break.

Except that it wasn't quite a break. As per the terms of the sale, Ishita was under a two-year lock-in wherein she would continue with Aegis BPO and its new acquisition as Chief Operating Officer.

This was to be her second and last stint as an employee in the corporate sector.

The second stint was not much of an improvement on her earlier one. She still chaffed at authority. She missed being her own boss. Worse, Essar was not a company where women were encouraged to reach top positions. It was an essentially male-dominated company, with a male-dominated culture, and for the men there, having her around probably put a constraint on them in terms of their language and behaviour.

Though she had been co-opted to join as the COO, after a point of time, they apparently began wondering what to do with her and even decided to put her in charge of Corporate Communications — a thought which did not find favour with Ishita.

Ishita did her mandatory two-year stint, spending the second year setting up a semi-entrepreneurial project for them, and then she quit. It was another turning point for her since working at Essar made her revisit all the reasons why she hated the corporate culture — the strait-jacketed working environment, no freedom to explore and expand her horizons, strict adherence to rules, and of course submission to authority which she was unused to, having grown accustomed to working on her own.

The frenetic activity of nurturing and expanding an enterprise had consumed her for 11 years and Ishita decided that it was time to take a break. It was time to recharge her batteries, time to introspect, to look around and see what else life had to offer.

Her love for adventure and new challenges, her zeal for starting something new however, remained her defining characteristic. Even in this period of relative calm, she got involved in a venture by Meenu Vadera, who had started a cab service run exclusively by women and for women.

The venture, Sakha Consulting Wings Pvt Ltd, provided employment to women from disadvantaged sections of society, providing them with the required skills to run a cab service. Ishita was, and still is, associated with the company in an advisory capacity.

The break was primarily meant for Ishita to spend time with her daughter Tara, whom she had finally managed to adopt after four years.

Ishita had proved time and again that it was possible to live a life removed from the conventional and the ordinary. You didn't necessarily have to mould yourself into other people's expectations of what you ought to be — not even from a sense of filial duty or obligation.

"There has been an overall view that I've broken norms, done unconventional things. I did shake the family with my thought processes. I showed them that there's an alternative way to live life and it's perfectly okay."

Deciding not to get married till quite late in life, much to her mother's anguish, was one of them. Her decision to adopt a baby only underlined that unique character of hers.

"When I planned to adopt a daughter, it did not go down well with parts of my family," though her immediate family, like her father, was very supportive.

The introduction of a baby into her life — which she was used to living on her own terms, being responsible only for herself — has predictably shaken up her schedule and in fact, her whole attitude to life.

She had doubts about whether she could bring up a baby on her own, with little surrounding support. Her priorities changed almost immediately with the arrival of Tara. She has had to give up all the pursuits that she loved — trekking, hiking and skiing — since Tara is too small to take part in those activities.

Her social life, meetings with friends, everything has taken a backseat. "Wherever she can't participate, I too cannot do those things. I've sacrificed all of that." She admits that it's a struggle to juggle all her responsibilities and that there are days when she wonders why she is doing all these things. "But I would not have it any other way."

Towards the end of the self-imposed break, Ishita started to fret. Her maternal instincts were finding fulfillment in bringing up her baby but her business and entrepreneurial instincts were not. "I was wondering what to do because I realised I couldn't sit at home. That wasn't me. It was not going to fulfil me. At the end of the day, I would sit back and think — what did I do today. I took care of Tara. I loved her to death, but it was not enough. I needed to be working."

An Entreprenur — Again!

In 2008, the United States was in the grip of a financial crisis triggered by the sub-prime mortgage crisis; Lehman Brothers had gone bust and a host of other iconic banks were to follow. Oil prices were soaring to record levels.

India felt the shock waves of that crisis and the last quarter of the calendar year 2008 and the first quarter of 2009 were among the worst quarters that the country ever faced, with consumer demand dipping, hitting sales of cars and other consumer products. The Indian government responded with two rounds of stimulus measures designed to boost the economy.

Automobile and retail sectors which were among the first to fall victims to the economic downturn were also the first to respond to the stimulus measures.

Retailers, especially apparel makers, were exploring options to sell their products, particularly excess inventory of stock and merchandise which they could not get rid of even at the end-of-season discount sales.

Anchal Jain, a close friend of Ishita, came up with the idea of launching a discounted retail venture — it was a concept that worked overseas, such as in the United States, and it would work here too.

Thus, 99labels.com was born. The company sells branded apparel and accessories — probably a line from the previous season — at a deeply discounted price, as the makers of these items want to get rid of excess merchandise.

"We are the liquidation company for their excess inventory." Her company sources the excess merchandise from these companies and sells it at a discount on her portal.

For Ishita, 99labels.com provided the challenge she was craving for. It was a new sector, a new model based on entirely new rules — she could write the rules. She and her co-founder Anchal researched the segment for six months before they plunged into it full-time.

"When I started it, I knew nothing about retail, or the online space or about a B2C venture. The idea appealed to me. I thought it had merit. It had a solid, simple premise to it."

The initial investment she made in the venture was also far greater this time — Rs 1 crore. The scale of operations was much larger than it had been in her previous venture. It was also more organised.

She had the benefit of prior experience and most of all, she was confident. Her previous success as an entrepreneur had given her that vital input.

This time, there was no disapproving family. In fact, her parents were proud of her, proud of her success.

Slightly more than two years old, 99labels.com is still in the early stages of its growth.

The company has already set up offices in Mumbai, Delhi, Paris and London, while Ishita is in the process of expanding and setting up stocking points.

The whole model is run on the premise that premium brands are left with excess inventory of a particular product line every season. Even end-of-season sales are not enough to move them off the shelves. While companies like Levi's, Reebok and some others do have factory outlets in certain locations, where they sell their excess inventory, many brands are loath to do that because it dilutes their brand equity.

Furthermore, they cannot discount it in their own outlets beyond a certain point, as that would hit sales of their fresh merchandise.

Also, in India, factory outlets are not so common given the high real estate costs. Makers of high-fashion labels would rather use precious real estate to set up full-priced stores rather than run a discounted outlet.

This is the gap that 99labels.com is filling. Ishita expects that with Foreign Direct Investment in single brand retail raised to 100 percent, there will be more premium brands entering India, thus generating more excess merchandise, which will then need such outlets to liquidate them.

The model also makes economic sense from a customer perspective because working women and men rarely have the time to go looking for branded labels. The online shopping format helps them indulge in hassle-free shopping from their homes, offices or wherever they may be, and that too at a steeply discounted price. The items they are buying may be from the season gone by, but this does not really matter to the mass affluent clientele that Ishita is targeting.

The portal also does brisk business in Tier 2 and Tier 3 cities where people aspire to wear branded clothes but do not have access to them for want of such outlets.

"It's a win-win proposition for all. Brands get to liquidate excess inventory, customers get to buy good brands at discounts, and we make our margins with the sales."

Margins in this particular kind of discounted format model are slightly lower than what a full-priced retailer would make. Ishita estimates margins in the region of 20 to 25 percent.

However, break-even is still some years away as e-commerce businesses take a long time to make profits. Scale and volumes will matter because as it grows larger, the company's ability to negotiate better prices from the apparel makers will also rise. "We can get better margins then."

Ishita, who raised funds from Info Edge last year, is again involved in raising funds afresh for her venture.

The venture is highly capital intensive, with salaries being the biggest chunk of the total costs. Good quality talent with specialised knowledge of retail, digital marketing aids and IT people to maintain smooth operations of the portal, all these come at a cost.

Since the company has to have inventory on stock at any given time, a continuous flow of working capital is needed.

Ishita says she got the timing right when she launched 99labels.com, because the industry was just coming out of a recession and companies had excess stock to sell. This coincided with a return in consumer interest as economic sentiments improved.

The portal has also begun receiving offers to sell fresh merchandise at discounted prices from some brands who want to test the market in India before they set up full-fledged stores here.

"The challenge in this is to take it to profitability and to create a market which does not even exist."

While Ishita is obviously thrilled with what is doing, she is simultaneously looking at the social entrepreneurship space, where she feels she has a lot to contribute. She also wants to mentor new entrepreneurs, teaching them what she had to learn on her own and guiding them through the pitfalls they are likely to face.

Routine bores her while challenges excite her to do her best. "My overriding trait is I want to learn new things. That's why I work well in start-ups."

And that's why life as an employee in a rule-bound corporate hierarchy once suffocated her.

"I'm happiest sitting in a small room, on a broken chair, trying to convert an idea into a reality."

4

THE PURVEYOR OF HEALTH AND BEAUTY

Vandana Luthra

Founder
VLCC Healthcare

When Vandana Luthra approached her rather conservative father-in-law with the idea of working and doing something on her own, he asked her, "What do you want to do?"

Vandana said, "I want to open a small wellness and beautycentre."

"What is that?"

"I'll be cutting people's hair..."

"A barber! You want to be a barber? My bahu (daughter-in-law) is going to be a barber!" Her father-in-law was almost scathing in his comments.

Vandana explained that she was not going to be a barber. She would provide a range of beauty services to people and that included skin care and hair cuts.

He was not very convinced and predicted that her venture would not last more than six months and that she would return to the family crying. Vandana said that she wanted to make a go of it, nevertheless.

Seeing that her mind was made up, he asked her what she wanted from him, and offered to advance her some money as capital. Vandana replied that she only wanted his blessings and turned down his offer of money.

With the backing of her husband, who procured a loan of Rs 1.5 lakh for her from State Bank of India, Vandana bought out a beauty salon in Delhi's upmarket Safdarjung enclave. The salon had belonged to a lady who wanted to sell it and move to Nepal. The shop was 2,000 square feet in size, and Vandana started off by offering beauty and slimming services in this first outlet.

Her father-in-law's dire prediction did not come true. That was in 1989. Today, Vandana Luthra's Curls and Curves, or as it is more easily recognised, VLCC Healthcare, has more than 300 centres spread across 109 cities in 9 countries including UAE, Oman, Bahrain, Qatar, Kuwait, Sri Lanka, Bangladesh and Nepal.

She is currently in talks to acquire a company in the UK and to open a centre in Cairo, Egypt. Also on the anvil is an initial public offering of shares, expected to be completed during the current financial year.

Vandana's decision to go into business on her own was made at an early age. As a young girl growing up, she hardly spent any time with her father, who would leave for work early in the morning and return home late at night. "I would not see him for days. So I made up my mind that I was not going to work for anybody. I would start my own business."

Her father did not take her pronouncements very seriously,

treating it as a passing fad. "When I would talk about starting my own business, he would say — 'She's not going to do it'. "

Vandana, however, remained steadfast in her purpose. By the time she graduated from college, she had already zeroed in on the beauty and health sectors as the areas she would focus on. As the events that followed showed, she pursued that idea with a single-minded dedication, ensuring that she got the right qualifications for it.

Even the delay that she faced in starting her business did not dim her ambitions. When the time was right and when she found she had sufficient time on hand, she plunged into her venture with the kind of steadfast purpose that characterised all her actions.

The beauty, fitness and healthcare market in India is highly fragmented, with most players in the segment being proprietor-owned boutique firms, largely driven by the brand equity of the founders. There are very few organised players in the segment. The sector itself is divided. Within the sector, there are those focused exclusively on beauty and there are others focused exclusively on fitness and nutrition.

The beauty industry in India is estimated to be worth close to Rs 8,000 crore, and growing at a compounded annual rate of 35 percent. The health and fitness industry is still to catch on and is currently worth slightly more than Rs 3,000 crore, though industry insiders estimate that the growth potential here is exponential, with the culture of fitness consciousness permeating the mass affluent, the biggest chunk of the consuming class.

Lakme of Hindustan Unilever and Kaya Skin Clinic owned Marico Industries cater to the beauty and skin care market and are two of the few corporate players in the segment. Talwalkar's runs India's largest chain of health clubs but it offers only fitness and nutrition services.

Then there are other smaller services run by specialists in their fields, like dermatologists, dieticians and nutritionists. Prominent among these are cosmetologist Rekha Sheth's Yuva clinic, Jamuna Pai's Blush clinics and Anjali Mukherjee's Health Total.

VLCC happens to be the only one straddling all the three areas — beauty, fitness and nutrition.

The Glamour-Struck Girl

Vandana Luthra was glamour-struck right from an early age. A television programme showing people getting facials and massages done would hold her in thrall, during her childhood days.

Of course, what she really wanted to be was an actor. Films and movies and the associated glamour appealed to her. She was deeply interested in theatre when she was still in school, and dabbled in plays as well.

Vandana was brought up in an upper middle-class family in Delhi, surrounded by the trappings of a corporate life, since her father was a director in German company Siemens and her mother was a socialite.

She was naturally bright but was an average student at school — unlike her brother who topped his class throughout his academic life — though she did make it to Lady Shriram College, where she graduated in Psychology.

While she was still in college, she took training in a beauty course from a polytechnic institute. However, acting still fascinated her. She tried to convince her father that she wanted to be an actor. She even got admission to the Film Institute in Pune, but her father was not happy with the idea. That was the first time he said no to the daughter whom he doted on. "I am not allowing you to go and live in Bombay."

She also got an acting offer from a film director when she turned 18, but her father was unyielding. Vandana opted not to go against her father's wishes and that idea was shelved. But the beauty bug was still alive within her.

"I was always interested in beauty. I wanted to be associated with glamour. I don't know why it was so important to me. I was also a health and fitness freak," says Vandana.

When she was a child, she was forever using and experimenting with her mother's make-up products and cosmetics. All her pocket money went into buying the best make-up that she could find.

She raided her mother's facial products and experimented by trying out waxing, pedicures and manicures, on herself and on her mother.

After graduating from college, she went to Germany, where she studied nutrition. But her interest was cosmetology, so she went onward to Paris and London to study and gain expertise in that area. When she started her beauty business in India, she decided to marry these streams and provide a holistic approach to looking good.

The beauty explosion in India is a very recent phenomenon. Earlier, the concept of beauty lay in acquiring a fairer complexion, and beauty products consisted largely of whitening creams like Afghan Snow, face powders, the rather low-key Lacto Calamine and bathing soaps led by Lux. Looking beautiful was strictly a woman's prerogative. Products for men were shaving creams or after-shave lotions, embodied by the enduring image of a virile man drenched in Old Spice in the TV commercials.

There were some foreign brands like Max Factor (now owned by Procter & Gamble) and Gala of London, but they were expensive and affordable only for a certain segment of the population. If you had relatives living overseas, you could get Oil of Olay, but those living in India had to be content with Himani in summer and Ponds in winter.

There were no anti-aging products then and personal grooming largely consisted of a good haircut, a facial and possibly a massage — at least for the middle classes — and all this came under the tag of luxuries to be indulged in once or twice a year.

In Training to Be a *Bahu*

Vandana did not immediately plunge into her business after completing her courses on beauty and nutrition.

When she was 16, she had met Mukesh, a friend of her brother's, who came from a business family. She fell in love with him. They dated for about five years and when she was 21 and he was 23, they married.

His family was against the marriage. They had plans of marrying off their son into another business family, and Vandana did not quite fit the bill of the kind of bride they were looking for, for their son.

Vandana had been brought up in a liberal and westernised atmosphere, where corporate parties were de rigueur.

"My husband's family was very conservative."

They expected a traditional *bahu* who would cook and clean and do all the usual household chores that a woman in India is expected to do.

"My journey has been one of transformation," says Luthra. "The kind of family I came from and the one I married into."

After her marriage, they moved into her husband's place — "a small *barsati* in Delhi" — where the newly married couple stayed on the ground floor while her husband's family lived on the top floor.

Vandana wanted to go to work immediately and her husband left the choice to her. But fate intervened. Three months into her marriage, she found herself pregnant with her first daughter.

Her priorities changed. She decided that she would put her plans for a career on the back-burner for a while. "I love children so I thought — let me have my baby and settle my family and then get to work."

It was eight years before she could finally get down to the task of starting on her venture. In the meanwhile, she had another daughter as well.

Vandana views those eight years as a big learning experience. Not only was she settling down and setting up a family, she also had to adjust to a totally new way of life.

"It was a total change of culture. I was from a non-vegetarian family and my in-laws were vegetarian. Not even eggs. Also, I had to wear a saree. I had never worn sarees before."

She also did not know how to cook. She confessed to her mother-in-law that she was totally ignorant about anything to do with domestic work.

"Don't you know anything? What did your mother teach you?" asked her mother-in-law.

"Well, she gave us an education," replied Vandana. "But I am willing to learn anything if you will teach me."

Vandana says she won over her inimical relatives-by-marriage with her willingness to learn everything and her flexible nature.

"I learnt to cook. I learned to sweep and mop the floor.

"It's very important for a woman to manage her home properly. If she cannot manage her home properly, how is she going to manage anything else in life?"

A very astute observation from a woman who says that now her home runs on remote control — a legion of household help controlled invisibly by her — as she glob-trots to manage and expand her business.

Vandana has rather strong views on the role of men and women in running a family and the household. Though she, in no way, considers herself inferior to men, she holds the opinion that a home is the woman's domain.

"Men cannot run a home. Absolutely not! Women are great managers. They can manage everything. A woman is much more capable than a man is, of managing and running things."

As a woman, Vandana always craved for a beautiful home of her own — "not necessarily luxurious or expensive" — but neat and comfortable. "I wanted to be a creator, to have a beautiful home and beautiful children." When it comes to her house, she's a perfectionist. "I keep my house very clean. I am a good cook. I can do everything on my own and hate to be dependent on anybody."

She's also irritated by her older daughter's untidy house. "I want to give her a piece of my mind. Why is her house so dirty? I've been busy for the last few days organising her house."

Most men, she generalises, hate to help around the house. "Men are very selfish. They will help, but only up to a point."

She attributes this to fundamental differences between men and women. "These differences will always be there, no matter how much people talk about all these things."

VLCC — An Idea that Became a Business

VLCC started off by offering beauty and slimming services. Gym equipment in those days was expensive and had to be imported, and the concept of 'gymming' was in itself not very popular.

A journalist friend helped her with a write-up in the Mumbai tabloid *MiD-DAY,* and she was launched.

Her first client (whom she doesn't want to name) was a celebrity, though she did not realise it until three years later.

Among her earliest clients was actor Dimple Kapadia, who used to visit a cousin who stayed nearby. And the word spread. She had the advantage of starting something unique and opening up a whole new world of beauty, with fitness thrown in, for those who could afford it and for those who wanted to look good.

Her clientele grew mostly by word of mouth from satisfied customers. In a few months, she opened her second centre in Safdarjung.

"It was totally sold out. I had a long waiting list." The place became well known, especially among well-heeled Delhi women, as also in other metros.

"If you want to build a brand, you have to be result-driven. Services have to meet consistently high standards, otherwise people are not going to keep coming," says Luthra.

Today, VLCC has positioned itself as a middle-class, affordable brand catering to the upwardly mobile, class-conscious, aspiring consumer segment which willingly spends more on looking good. "I've always believed that if we keep ourselves affordable, it will lead to more footfalls and the visibility of the brands will also be higher. I feel that the success of any brand will depend on its appeal to the middle classes."

Vandana's philosophy is to make her customers happy. She attributes her success to this belief and to the fact that the people working in the company have a sense of ownership. Employees are offered bonuses and incentives for achieving targets.

Targets are set for every month and the team at VLCC is motivated to achieve them.

When Vandana started out, she had a team of 12 people; now the company employs more than 6,000 people across India and overseas.

It was not smooth sailing all the way. Success, especially that of a woman, creates strange bedfellows, to use a cliché.

Luthra admits to having been swindled by a friend of her husband's, who somehow inveigled his way into a partnership with her.

"When I opened my fourth centre in Mumbai, I got stuck with a person who became a business partner without investing anything in the venture." He promised to help her open a centre on Linking Road, a busy stretch of road extending from Bandra to Khar in the western suburbs of Mumbai, but eventually she had to open one in Chembur in the eastern suburbs. She had to work hard to attract customers to her shop.

Once the outlet was running successfully, the gentleman in question demanded that either he be given 50 percent-partnership in the venture or she should get out of the centre altogether. "My husband told me not to fight and to give him what he wanted."

The two went on to open many centres in Mumbai. By that time, VLCC Healthcare was starting to attract attention from private equity and other strategic investors. In 2004, brokerage and private investment firm CLSA picked up 13.65 percent stake in the company for about $15 million. Everstone Capital had already taken a 15 percent share in the company earlier. The investors weren't happy with the joint venture structure, and the partnership split.

"It created a lot of bad blood," says Luthra.

VLCC bought back CLSA's stake in 2011, when its investment term in the company ended. At present, about 85 percent of the ownership is in the hands of Vandana and her husband Mukesh, who handles the financial part of the business.

Vandana has taken on the role of a mentor in the organisation now. "The company is professionally driven. We have heads of businesses who take all the operational decisions now. My focus is more on research and development and technical training."

Vandana is also busy with her expansion plans. Planning for the company's maiden issue of equity shares is on her mind and it looks like a reluctant exercise. Recently, the company raised Rs 200 crore for expansion, so it doesn't really require funds. It has financed itself via the mezzanine funding route and a part of this will be converted into equity at the time of the IPO.

"I am very reluctant. We don't need the money. I don't want to be answerable to people. But then, I realise that we need to climb to a totally different level." She says the actual amount to be raised via the IPO will be decided closer to the issue date.

VLCC has tied up with Florida-based Pritikin to launch Medical Spas — health and weight-loss centres for the obese and those struggling to lose weight. These centres will be located on the outskirts of big cities, such as on the Pune-Mumbai expressway or outside Delhi. There are also plans to start hair-zones inside malls.

The money raised will go into VLCC's health business and its educational ventures — to campuses, institutes, domestic and international businesses. The company, however, generates a lot of cash, and the expansions are sustained by these internal accruals. The company has earmarked around Rs 100 crore in the current year for its expansion plans.

Along with her business, Vandana is expanding the reach of the industry as well. "We are the pioneers in the wellness and healthcare industry. We are helping the industry to grow."

In 2001, she set up the VLCC Institute of Beauty and Nutrition, which now has 51 campuses in 39 cities and offers specialised courses in beauty, hair cosmetology, make-up, spa therapies and nutrition.

'Now companies like Kaya, Jawed Habib... they take on students from our institute. I'm helping to organise the industry. You'll see a lot of players entering the industry now and I'll help with that."

"I feel like the mother of the industry," she says rather expansively.

Vandana has given a new definition to the often-used and rather clichéd phrase, 'beauty with a purpose.'

Vandana Luthra and her company are working to improve the lives of underprivileged sections of the population. They are engaged with several non-government organisations and the Ministry of Women and Child Development to provide vocational training to women in rural areas to make them financially independent.

The VLCC Foundation runs programmes to provide health

and education support to the underprivileged. It also aids rehabilitation schemes for the physically challenged. It regularly organises health check-up camps that offer services related to cardiology, gynecology and diabetes, among others.

There are a number of organisations the foundation supports, to promote the education of disabled and destitute children. Amar Jyoti and Tamanna are two such initiatives. Vandana is actively involved in the funding of Khushii, an NGO outfit led by former cricketer Kapil Dev.

The road ahead for Vandana presents still more challenges.

Succession is an issue, with both her daughters not following her into the business.

"I don't have a great succession plan because my (younger) daughter wants to practice law. And I don't want to come in her way. Let her do what she wants."

Her elder daughter is busy raising her family. "I respect them for what they have chosen — because I feel family is important for a woman."

She says that this is the reason she needs to make sure that the company is professionally run. "So my husband and I have to make an exit."

With her older daughter moving to London, there are hopes that she will finally look after the UK unit of the company, which will soon be operational.

She reveals that a lot of people and companies have made offers to buy out VLCC. "But I'm not going to sell. I can never sell my company, my child."

As for herself, she says, "I am 53 now and I'm going to keep on working."

5

A LAWYER BY OSMOSIS

Zia Mody

Co-founder and Partner
AZB & Partners

It is always hard to follow a superlative act, especially when that act belongs to your larger-than-life father.

Zia Mody, the oldest child and only daughter of Soli Sorabjee, and one of the founding partners of prestigious Indian corporate law firm AZB Partners, grew up in an atmosphere where discussion of legal cases at the dinner table was the norm. It was inevitable, given that her father was such a high profile lawyer.

Soli Sorabjee, the former Attorney General of India, is a household name in the country. He was Attorney General for six years, from 1998 to 2004, and prior to that he was the Solicitor General.

Author of several books, Sorabjee has a formidable reputation and has been involved in several high profile cases in the country.

"I got into law by osmosis, just because of this very powerful figure in our lives," says Zia.

The children were used to their father holding lengthy conversations over the telephone, while at dinner, talking to his solicitors about his next day's work. He also used walkie-talkies sometimes, to conduct his conversations.

All that the children would hear was their father's side of these long conversations, "which were always agitated, very intense." It all sounded exciting and interesting to young Zia at that time.

Soli had a love for Shakespeare's works, was keen on English literature, and was a jazz enthusiast as well. The children didn't necessarily share his love for all these things, but "we got a good dose of it all," says Zia.

Zia's mother Zena describes her daughter as being very argumentative as a child. "So I thought that (law) was the profession that would suit her best. She was determined from the very beginning that she was going to be a lawyer."

Due to the nature of his work, Soli Sorabjee was often absent from home, flying down to Delhi where he spent the whole week, and then returning home for the weekends. While he was always this overwhelming figure in the background, it was left to Zena to bring up the children, and she was a strong influence in their lives and in their choice of careers.

Zia was the eldest child, but Jehangir, next in line and the oldest boy, wanted to be a lawyer as well. "He wasn't sure whether he wanted to take up law or medicine," says Zena.

With one towering lawyer in the family and one of the children (Zia) also taking up law, what the family needed was a doctor. "I always used to joke — my husband is a hypochondriac; we need a doctor in the family. So Jehangir obliged and became the doctor."

Jehangir, who is a consulting physician at Bombay Hospital,

likes to say his mother pushed him into medicine. "The choice was his," his mother laughs. She admits that he would have made a successful lawyer as well, because he had an aptitude for both.

Her other children are Jamsheed and the youngest Hormazd, automobile enthusiast and editor of Autocar India.

Zia was brought up in a liberal atmosphere where the concept of gender bias was virtually unknown. She was a high achiever right since her school days, driven by her ambitious parents, especially her mother, who wanted her children to excel in whatever they did.

"You know, alpha mothers lead to alpha daughters and so on."

Zia was born in 1956, in Mumbai, and did her schooling in J. B. Petit High School for Girls. "By the time I passed out of school and got into college, I had set my sights on the legal profession."

Once it was decided that Zia was to be a lawyer, her course was pretty well charted out.

She was sent abroad to study law. She went to Selwyn College, Cambridge University, UK for her law degree and then she got her LLM from Harvard University in the US. She was overseas for about 10 years and she missed a lot of what was happening back home.

The decade of the 1970s opened with Indira Gandhi storming to power on the Garibi Hatao (Remove Poverty) platform. Banks, coal mines and the insurance sector were all nationalised. India won a war against Pakistan, leading to the creation of Bangladesh.

Though the economic conditions of the Indians had not improved, there was a general 'feel good' atmosphere all around. Then came the oil crisis in 1973, and following that, in May 1974, the 20-day strike by 17 million workers of the Indian Railways, which paralyzed the movement of goods and people across the country.

Indira Gandhi brutally suppressed the strike and imposed Emergency.

Zia was not in India then, but she knew that her father was going through a stressful phase. "People were worried whether lawyers or anyone else would be arrested. It got really tense. I know Dad went through tough times."

Being in the UK and US also meant that she missed out on the gender problem that she would otherwise have had to encounter, if she had started working here in India.

Zia did not immediately return to India after passing her Bar exams. For one, since she had been educated overseas, it seemed natural to practice in a country where she felt more comfortable. For another, opportunities in India during those days were very few, especially for a young, aspiring woman, in the legal field.

She stayed on in New York — a city which she loved and still has a lot of affection for — where she joined the prestigious corporate law firm Baker & McKenzie. She worked with the firm for about five years, honing her skills in advising businesses.

In 1984, Zia decided to return to India to get married.

India, in 1984, was growing at the Hindu rate of growth, and liberalisation was still some years away. In many ways, that was a watershed year in the Indian polity, marking as it did, the assassination of Indira Gandhi and the entry of her eldest son Rajiv Gandhi into politics, with the latter bringing youth, optimism, and fresh ways of thinking to the moribund economy, still ruled by stodgy politicians of another era.

Zia was not even sure that she wanted to get back to India. Her father strongly advised her against it, concerned that the change and the cultural shift would be too much for her to handle, that she would not enjoy it and might fall into depression. "He told me to think very carefully."

However, once Zia had made up her mind, there was no dithering and she came back to India. "I was set on getting married. So I had to come back."

A Barrister in the Indian Courts

She had no immediate thoughts of setting up a corporate law firm at that time, because in the mid-80s, there was very little foreign direct investment and corporate takeovers were few and far between. She started a litigation practice of her own — under the banner Chambers of Zia Mody (CZM) — and for nearly 10 years after she returned, she was just a barrister practicing in the Bombay High Court.

In Indian courts today, women lawyers still tend to attract attention. In the '80s, it must have been a novelty. Zia admits that she struggled with gender discrimination during her early days, when she was a counsel practicing in the Indian courts.

Though she glosses over those early days of struggle, she admits that insecurities and uncertainty were her companions. Getting clients was hard. Convincing them that she could do the job as well as any man would, was harder. She was always being tested. And she always had to fare better than her male peers did, when handling cases.

There was no help to be had. She kept her head down and went on with it. It certainly was a culture shock for her. From New York City to Mumbai was a big jump. "It was very different," Zia says, when asked about the shift. In America, you had your own room, your own secretary." In Mumbai, she had to make do with half a desk shared with someone else, no secretaries, no infrastructure. It was a different world that she had to adjust to.

"For 10 years, I just put on my band and gown and went to practise." She had a lot of passion but no credibility yet, and nobody was willing to take chances on a young, untried woman. "I couldn't take my brief for granted. It came with a lot of hard work."

The hard work which characterised her early days is something that has taken on legendary proportions now — at least in corporate legal circles. Zia still keeps a punishing schedule, starting work on most days at 10 a.m. in the morning, and returning home often after 2 a.m. in the night.

There were very few women practicing in the courts at that time. It was both challenging and exciting, struggling to make a name for herself as a person and combating the gender prejudice.

"There was a lot of nervousness within the court room. Of course, a 60-year-old businessman is wondering what a young woman aged 25 or 30 is doing representing him."

She grabbed each opportunity with intensity and tried to prove herself every step of the way. Her struggle also included making seniors believe that she was a diligent junior, convincing judges that she was sincere, and assuring clients that she was working hard on their behalf and would be there for them.

"My father always used to say that you should pray that your senior doesn't show up for the matter, so you can handle it."

The struggle to prove her worth lasted about 3 to 4 years, after which the intensity lessened, as she had reasonably established her reputation by then. Along the way, she also represented for free the Bombay Environmental Action Group, headed by the late Shyam Chainani, who was crusading against violations in the construction sector and the threat these posed to the city's creaky urban infrastructure.

Then in 1991, India ushered in the winds of liberalisation in the economy. Zia was enjoying her practice but she also wanted to do something else.

She had several options open to her at that point. Her father was a well-known and respected figure in legal circles. She could have followed in his footsteps and wound up working for the government and in the Supreme Court. Indeed, that was what Soli wanted for her.

She could join another law firm, she would easily be snapped up considering her education, experience and pedigree. But the snag here was that she would be a junior partner in the firm and would have to work her way up, with no guarantee that she would ever reach the top, considering the prejudices at work in the Indian social fabric.

Or she could start her own corporate law firm.

Z for Zia

Zia chose the third option. "We started off with a motley team of around 10 to 12 lawyers."

This was a move which irked Soli. He was disappointed. He wanted her to follow in his footsteps and ultimately get to the Supreme Court. But corporate law was where Zia had had her grounding and it was an area that she knew very well and was comfortable with.

It was not an easy ride, though it was fun with all the teamwork amongst the lawyers in her firm. Zia remembers it as working long hours into the night, learning new things every day, keeping pace with changing laws. Today, AZB has about 17 partners and employs about 250 lawyers, whom Zia describes as a fabulous set of people.

AZB comes from the first alphabets of the names of the three founding partners. A for Ajay Bahl, Z for Zia and B for Bahram Vakil. Her original CZM metamorphosed into AZB as each of the partners joined.

Among their first foreign clients was mutual fund firm Alliance Capital, to whom they were advisors in setting up their operations in India. "We were treading new ground. Clarifications were required on a daily basis. We often had to deal with issues that were not clearly defined."

Alliance Capital led to more international clients. In the beginning — probably due to her education, her overseas work experience and the friends who referred them — her clientele was largely (almost 90 percent) from the US and UK. Currently, it is almost equally split between Indian and foreign companies.

Her reputation spread by word of mouth in the small world of corporate legal firms. "We couldn't get enough sleep, we couldn't even find time to go to the bathroom. We just worked... and worked... and worked."

While Zia doesn't remember the first merger and acquisition transaction she handled, her favourite was when the Tatas acquired Singapore-based NatSteel Holdings in 2004, for $486.4 million. "I liked that one. It was my first exposure to so many foreign jurisdictions, dealing with so many different laws, making sure the client was fully protected."

At present, AZB & Partners has become the go-to law firm for cross border mergers, takeovers and fund raising programmes. In the acquisition of Cairn Energy's India unit by UK-based miner Vedanta Resources, her firm was the advisor to London-listed Vedanta on Indian legal regulations.

How she got the Vedanta mandate was extremely fortuitous. Zia met Vedanta's Anil Agarwal at Heathrow Airport while both of them were waiting for a flight to Mumbai, and the two fell into conversation. Zia's brother, Jehangir happened to be Agarwal's doctor. Some days later, back in India, he called her to ask for her help with the deal.

Her firm advised Bharti Airtel on its $10.7 billion acquisition of Zain's African operations from MTC Telecommunication.

More recently, it was appointed as the sole legal advisor in the merger of Tech Mahindra with Mahindra Satyam — erstwhile Satyam Computer, whose founder Ramalinga Raju is being prosecuted in Indian courts for accounting frauds and forgeries committed while at the helm of the company.

The Tatas are a loyal client, AZB having been involved in two of the group's high profile, cross-border purchases — Tata Steel's $12 billion Corus deal in 2007 and Tata Motors' $2.3 billion buy-out of UK-based luxury car-maker Jaguar and Land Rover in the same year.

The firm's other notable deals are Aditya Birla's $6 billion purchase of Novelis and Reliance Industries' $7.2 billion deal with British Petroleum.

AZB & Partners has expertise in a wide range of corporate transactions including takeovers, fund raising, initial public offerings, mergers, dispute resolution, insurance and project finance.

In 2010, the company had advised Reliance Industries on its $1.5 billion bond issuance.

When she started off on her own, she was still practicing in the Indian courts, but then she realised that if she had to make the venture a success, she had to devote her time to it exclusively, and that her corporate law practice could not be a part-time venture.

Talking about the steep rise to get to the top, Zia says it was hard work all the way. "In the first 10 years, we were just building up the firm and our name." She gives full credit to the entire team of lawyers who, working around the clock, made it all happen.

"But it was so, so stressful. We were worried in case we missed anything. The Internet did not have as much information then as it has today. All the time we were wondering whether our sources were right and whether the previous night something had happened, which we did not know about in the morning." It was as if, during those days, time was their mortal enemy.

Being Soli Sorabjee's daughter did go a little way towards getting her the required attention and clients, especially among the Indian corporates.

But initially, all her clients were from overseas and they did not really relate to her second name. By that time, Zia was already married to Indian real estate tycoon Jaydev M Mody, who belonged to the Piramal family which owns Peninsula Land, and she had changed her surname.

Her first daughter was born in 1986.

She admits that she has no work-life balance. It was all work and she regrets it. She felt guilty but helpless about not being able to do anything about it as work claimed her. She had a supportive husband and in-laws who helped in taking care of her three daughters as they grew up. She says that with the supporting infrastructure, it all worked out in the end — but sometimes children need only their mothers.

"Guilt never goes away. It's part of being a young mother. You have to accept that. You are always balancing, rebalancing, multitasking, wrongly prioritising, killing yourself for wrongly prioritising."

Not being there for a special function, unable to be present during a critical exam, being busy at a conference when her daughters wanted to share something with her — Zia tried to minimise these lapses as much as she could and tried making up for it later. "But it is never enough."

Work was her passion and it always got top priority in her life. And because she had worked so hard to get to where she was and had achieved so much, she did not want to let go of all that. But second to work, family was priority, and she tried a juggling act with both. "Therefore, you screwed up sometimes at work and you screwed up sometimes at home," she says.

When Zia entered the legal profession in India, there were very few women. Today, more women are entering the profession since there are more opportunities and it also pays better. But law firms do lose a lot of women employees after a duration 10 to 12 years, due to marriage, children, guilt, stress, and when these women follow their husbands in case of a transfer.

Zia is at the forefront when it comes to pushing the cause of women and nurturing them in her firm. She realises that women struggle against so many things in life, that work and making a career for themselves gets very little priority in the process. She makes sure that women attorneys in her law firm get the same kind of opportunities that men do, but it is not always that easy.

When there are deals happening, lawyers working on the case have to be there day and night, and many women are not able to devote that kind of time due to their other commitments at home.

Currently, more than 40 percent of the lawyers employed in her firm are women.

"The reason why there are so few women at the top in the legal profession is that it's tough, very time-intensive, requires reading all the time and constant engagement with clients. It's not easy."

Zia herself has a reputation for meticulously going through all the drafts when working on a deal. It is this intense reading and minute attention to details that gives her an edge over many of her peers.

Many women are not able to give up some of their creature comforts or don't find it worthwhile giving up a lot for that hard work.

She is, of course, the first to admit that she got a better start in life than most other women. She didn't have to worry about finances and about getting the best of education. "But there are women who are not so privileged. They have a harder time of it."

Being a woman in the rarefied field of corporate law has also been advantageous in some ways. "I think I can get away with a lot more with my counterpart because I am a woman. I think there is a fair bit of additional chemistry which is non-combative."

She laments that there are fewer good law firms in India than one would expect from a country of this size. There is a lot of demand for talented lawyers because there are so few of them graduating from the schools. "I don't think you would get more than 500 to 600 lawyers from all over India who are from good schools."

In an interview last year with a financial newspaper, she said that quality would become critical with competition rising as more law firms entered the arena. "I think that there will be a clearer focus on specific practice domains that will require much more expertise, say for example, competition law."

At present, Zia has stopped getting involved in day-to-day execution of deals, leaving her younger and junior partners to handle them. But she still lends her vast expertise to at least 200 to 300 cases in a year, when her younger partners seek her advice.

Zia is not entirely uni-dimensional, although it's obvious that it's her legal work which defines her and still fires her up.

When she was younger, horse-riding used to be one of her interests. She tried to make time for it though she could not really pursue it as she would have liked.

Dancing — Bharatanatyam — was another interest that she took up during her earlier years, though again she could not really stick with it. Not so surprisingly perhaps, Zia also had an avid interest in cooking, and would attend Tarla Dalal's cooking classes.

Zia likes to travel, watch romantic movies ("and shed tears"), read books and listen to music. She catches up on her music and movies while on flights. In fact, she also has a distinction from the Royal College of Music.

Zia is a Parsi but follows the Baha'i Faith. The Baha'i Faith is relatively new, compared to other religions such as Islam, Christianity or even Zoroastrianism. It was founded about a century and a half ago by Baha'u'llah, a nobleman of Persian origin from Teheran. In the mid-19th century, he left his life of princely comfort and ease, and much like Gautama Buddha, went out to spread his message of peace and unity, enduring a lot of deprivation and persecution in the process.

The Baha'i Faith is a strong advocate of equality between the sexes.

"It's one of our religious principles that men and women are equal. In fact, our prophet goes on to say that if you have money only to educate one, then you must educate the woman or the girl child as she is the mother of future generations. This is there in writing and is part of our religious scriptures," says Zia.

Zia has given her daughters total freedom to pursue their lives and careers as they see fit. Though she would have liked to see them come into the legal profession and probably work in her firm, she has refrained from imposing anything on them.

Her obsession with her work and the fact that she could spend so little time with her daughters may be a reason why two of her daughters have decided to stay away from the legal profession. Only one of her daughters — the youngest one — is following in her footsteps.

She still has about five years to go before she retires, after which she plans to spend more time with her family and also do more work for her religious faith.

"I am very involved in the Baha'i religion. I don't do as much as I should and I really should be doing much more."

There are also plans for a merger of her law firm with another, to get access to a specific domain expertise.

Meanwhile, there is the next deal to look forward to.

6

FILLING IN THE BLANKS

Uma Ganesh

Founder and CEO
Global Talent Track

The education system in India, right from the primary school stage to higher levels, is less than ideal in terms of what is taught, the way it is taught and what students learn. The accent is not on learning, rather it emphasises 'maximising' examination scores. "How to crack that exam" is the leit motif for most students, and this is the reason why we have a rampant culture of coaching classes and tutorials in the country.

India has some of the best universities — many of them boasting of world class standards of education — but students merely use them as stepping stones to get into engineering colleges and

81

management institutes. The subjects being taught at the universities, in themselves hold little value.

When the Indian government set up the premium engineering institutes in India, specifically the Indian Institutes of Technology (IITs), they were supposed to be centres of excellence producing an elite group of top-notch engineers, who would be deployed in the manufacturing sector and industry, to power the growth of the economy.

Unfortunately, the pressures of getting a job and intense competition in the employment market have led to a climate where 'coaching classes' and 'guide books' help students get marks in the entrance examinations mostly through a system of rote and practice, without actually having understood the concepts. The tutorials and guides do all the groundwork; the students merely have to memorise and follow the steps and reproduce it in the various examinations that they take.

It is much like an automobile driving instructor teaching a student that the clutch has to be pressed before engaging the gear, without explaining the function of the clutch in the process.

Last year Co-founder and Chief Mentor of Infosys Technologies, Narayana Murthy created a furore when he said that the quality of candidates entering the IITs was deteriorating as the coaching classes were merely preparing aspirants to top the merit list and were not inculcating in them the spirit of acquiring knowledge. His comment that only 25 percent of the engineering graduates were readily employable led to even more heart-burn, with several sections of government, the coaching industry and some former IIT alumni coming down on him heavily for his uncharitable remarks.

Minister of State for HRD and External Affairs, Mr E. Ahmed extrapolated on the comment to include graduates from all institutes and universities.

Uncharitable, unfair, disappointing — we can choose to label his observation however we like, but the fact remains that getting good, talented people is the biggest challenge facing corporate India today. Among a nation of 1.2 billion people, only a small portion can be employed without any prior training.

The shortage of employability is a good reason why software companies have to spend a lot of time and money on 'training' engineers who have been recruited from campuses.

It is to bridge this gap in the requirement of 'employable' people that Uma Ganesh set up Global Talent Track. Uma, who has had extensive experience working in the field of education and in the technology sector, decided to transform her passion for education into something that would help society and industry. Global Talent Track works with state governments, universities, polytechnic institutes and corporates in making students graduating from colleges, universities and institutes 'employable'.

It was set up around three years ago with the backing of venture funds and other investors.

The resources that go into the venture are huge — as humongous as the universe she is targeting, which comprises the students who pour out of engineering colleges and other institutes, eager to get into well-paying jobs.

The idea for her education training venture came from her own experiences with industry, where the frequent lament of CEOs was — 'The business is there, I can get customers, I can get contracts and I can find markets (to sell my products). Only if I can find the talent and the right people to do the job'.

"Hearing that ad nauseum, I felt that we had to do something about this."

Global Talent Track, in a nutshell, is all about making young people employable.

The Learning Curve

This is not Uma's first brush with education. She has had previous stints with NIIT and Aptech — both pioneers in software education, which were set up at a time when computerisation in India had barely begun. They are credited with having created the demand for Information Technology professionals in India at a time when offices were still investing in typewriters.

Born in Bhopal, Uma was the eldest daughter of five children. She spent her childhood and adolescent years in Pondicherry and was brought up in a very liberal and free-thinking Tamil household, by an indulgent father, and a strict, and often autocratic, mother. The mother enforced discipline and a sense of duty among the children while the father encouraged them to experiment and try their hand at everything. Both wanted their children to excel at whatever they did.

The children were exposed to a rich blend of culture and philosophy, and Uma herself developed a keen interest in all things artistic, including Carnatic music. She was also an active member of the National Cadet Corps, pursuing it right into her college days.

In college, Uma took up Economics as her primary subject, and was one of the few students to actually opt for the subject. There was one major reason for this and it decided her future course of action. Her parents — like most parents during those days — wanted their daughter to join the Indian Administrative Services (IAS). Uma did not have any particular ambition of her own at that time and she thought that if she had to take the Civil Services exam, Economics would be the right subject for her.

While studying Economics, it dawned on her that IAS was not her calling, and that business education appealed to her more. So shelving the plan to enter the civil services to join the vast ranks of the bureaucracy in India, Uma decided to take up management studies.

It seems rather incredible now, when information is available to us at the touch of a button, but in the '70s, it was a tedious task for a small-town person who wanted to investigate the options available to study management. Uma had not heard of the Indian Institutes of Management — "Nobody in my family had heard of business education... and hardly anyone in my college knew anything about it or had pursued management studies. Anyway, I decided to apply to all the schools I knew and that my friends had heard of."

She got a call from all the three institutes she applied to and chose Faculty of Management Studies (FMS) in Delhi. It was a big step for Uma, going from the quiet environs of Pondicherry to the big, bustling capital of India.

"I learned a lot in FMS — from my professors, peers, and friends, because there were a lot of students who were from the IITs and other top colleges across the country. I really felt this was a place where I would learn a lot and I could also gauge where I stood and how much I could challenge myself in terms of learning."

Her very first job, after passing out from FMS, was with the then Grindlays Bank in Mumbai — a coveted job at that time.

It didn't take long for her to get disillusioned as all that she was doing was signing cheques and other routine banking chores. This was not why she had got her Diploma in Marketing. So one day, three weeks after joining Grindlays, instead of taking the bus all the way to the bank's office, she got off at the Crompton Greaves office and told the personnel manager there that she was joining them. Crompton had made her an offer during campus recruitments and the HR manager had kept in touch thereafter.

She spent the next five years in the power equipment firm Crompton Greaves, working in Mumbai, Chennai and Nasik, doing hard-core sales and marketing for the company. At Crompton, she met and married Ganesh Natarajan, whom we know today as Founder of mid-sized software firm Zensar Technologies. They had joined the company on the same day, and had corresponded regularly while he was posted in Nasik. She moved there when they decided to get married.

It was a steep learning curve for Uma at Crompton Greaves, both in terms of marketing and by virtue of being the only woman Management Trainee there.

"...There, in doses, I understood the distribution process, pricing process and back-end process. It gave me exposure to various aspects of business management other than marketing. It prepared me for my future career — learning inventory management, accounting, management information systems, being part of the factory system and product management." It also gave her, her first exposure to the use of technology in the workplace.

Her other major learning was how to deal with people (men mostly) who were hostile towards her simply because she was a woman. Uma relates the incident of a factory supervisor whom she needed to approach to get some data. The supervisor, who had risen from the ranks, refused to give her the information on some pretext or the other. When Uma went to her boss with the grievance, he told her, "That's your job, you have to get the data from him."

"So I went back to the supervisor and asked him again, and he said something rude to me. I cried over it and started to wonder whether there was anything in my behaviour that I could change, or whether I could approach the matter differently." Eventually, Uma did get the information, but it was a painful learning process she had to go through.

Her interactions with dealers, who were not used to female Sales Executives, sometimes bordered on the farcical.

She had to persuade one of her bosses, who was reluctant to send her out on field assignments, to allow her to meet with dealers.

So, Uma was sent to Tirunelveli to meet with one of Crompton's dealers there, and find out why he had such a poor record in selling the company's exhaust fans. There, she found that the dealer had a huge market for television sets — as people there were addicted to Tamil programmes broadcast by Sri Lanka Rupavahini TV Corporation — and hence, he had no interest in selling fans.

The dealer had another outlet in Tuticorin where, he said, she could try her luck and push her fans.

"How do I get there (Tuticorin)?" asked Uma.

The dealer replied, "You are a sales person, right? Here is my scooter — use this to get to Tuticorin."

Uma was crushed. "I couldn't ride a scooter. I felt so sheepish. I was waiting there thinking about how to get to Tuticorin. Do I take a bus? I realised I was asking him these basic questions."

It hit her that as a sales executive, she had to be resourceful in such matters. "So that was one lesson learnt."

She had another bizarre experience, this time in Madurai, where the dealer had already been told that Uma would be arriving there to discuss 'business' with him and that he had to take care of her. No woman had ever been there before to talk about the business with him.

Uma narrates, "I arrived at Madurai railway station in the morning. He (the dealer) was there to receive me at the station. We came out and then he hired an auto. He put me alone in one auto, he himself sat in another auto and then he took me to the hotel.

"He told me to take rest as his shop would open only at 10.30 a.m. and assured me that someone would come by to pick me up. And at the appointed time, someone came." And so the pattern was established. The person who came to pick her up would seat her alone in one auto and accompany her in another auto to the dealer's shop.

After discussing business at lunch time, the dealer would take her to a vegetarian restaurant — again one auto for her and another one for him. At the restaurant, he would seat her, go up to the cashier and order him to 'feed the lady' while he waited outside in the auto. It was unthinkable for the dealer to share the same auto or table with a woman.

"Those were the kind of challenges I had to face. People would tell me — 'You are not wanted there. Do you still want to go?' And I would say — 'Yes, I really want to go.' I never said no to anything." Uma says she got through it all by adapting to each situation and not letting the prejudices her gender created weigh her down.

After almost five years in Crompton, her husband Ganesh got an exciting break in Mumbai, in the Information Technology sector. Uma, who did not foresee too much of a future for herself in Crompton Greaves, also decided to move to the financial capital, where she was sure to have more opportunities.

And sure enough, she got a job as Territory Sales Manager in Modi Xerox, selling photo-copiers and other office equipment to corporates.

By then, Uma had become comfortable in a sales role. It also helped that the people she reported to in the organisation treated both men and women sales personnel as equals. Their job was to increase the sales of the company and that was the bottomline. "The learning was that we had to do our job by hook or crook."

Uma says that when she is called on now, to give lectures on marketing to young executives, especially women, she tells them that they should start off their career in sales. "Everything else you'll learn, but sales is something unique. If you don't do it in the early part of your life, you'll miss out on all the nuances. It helps you later, when you become a Sales Manager (which is different from being a Sales Executive), and you understand the dynamics of the situation."

"I strongly encourage MBA recruits that they better start their career selling — irrespective of where they want to be eventually." During this time, Uma had had her daughter, and since she was very focused on her career, the baby was being brought up by her parents. When her daughter was around two years old, both parents felt that it was time they took responsibility for their child.

Uma then decided to take a break from a full-time job and look after her daughter, though she also wanted to do something part-time on her own. She took to doing freelance assignments, advising small firms on how to prepare for automation and helping them set up computer and network systems. "They were all small assignments but it ensured that I did not lose my potential to earn."

When Ganesh's mother came to stay with them, Uma joined a company called FGP as Information Systems Manager.

Uma's husband, who was then Mumbai's Regional Head in NIIT, was called to Delhi, to head their Corporate Business division. Uma was happy in FGP, but NIIT made her an offer to manage their Career Education division, also in Delhi.

NIIT Ltd proved a turning point in Uma's career and was instrumental in pushing her towards the education sector. The company was involved in computer education but she realised the vast amount of work that needed to be done in the field of education per se, and how technology could be adeptly used in imparting education in an interesting and interactive way.

"I had no prior experience in education. I had no clue what this whole private sector business of education in computers was about, but NIIT felt that I could do it."

She was at NIIT for a relatively short time but it taught her a lot. The company was then still in its early stages of evolution, but contributing to the growth of the industry at the same time. Uma got progressively more involved, as the company introduced new products, created novel methods of delivering learning to students, and managed and marketed these products.

Being a pioneer in the field of computer education, NIIT attracted a lot of talent from top schools, as students came in droves to be taught basic and advanced computer skills. Corporates were also utilizing its services to upgrade and impart new skills to their employees.

After about a year and a half there, the husband-wife duo was lured by another IT education firm Aptech Ltd, back to Mumbai. Uma was initially given the job of expanding the education centres and adding new products to their basket. Thereafter, she was moved to Business Transformations and from that to handling international business.

All this added to Uma's store of knowledge on the education sector and delivery strategies.

From Aptech, she moved to Zee Interactive Learning Systems, Subhash Chandra's education venture. It was virtually an entrepreneurial role. When she joined the company, it was just about two years old.

Zee gave her an understanding of a completely new medium and the ability to reach out everywhere. "NIIT and Aptech gave me large doses of technology and its use in education. Zee taught me about the delivery of education over television and that gradually gave way to the use of the computer."

At Zee, she was responsible for the profit and loss account — right from generating revenues, to finding their office space and getting people. "I was part of a large corporate entity and this was an independent, separate division within that."

Uma spent seven years with Zee Interactive from 1995 to 2001, at the end of which she took another sabbatical — this time to do a doctorate course in management from IIT, Mumbai.

Next, she created a boutique firm for e-learning and ran that for three years in India. As part of that phase, she later moved to the United Kingdom and did some work on education with

Greenwich University. "That gave me an opportunity to interact with young learners from other parts of the world." She also wrote a book based on her PhD thesis and on her previous work experiences in industry.

She spent a year and a half with the management executive team of Hong Kong and Shanghai Banking Corporation (HSBC), which wanted her to expand their base of operations in India and guide them on what they needed to do to tap outsourcing opportunities.

Of her years in the UK and at HSBC, Uma says, "They were important to me in terms of the insights they gave me to develop the business plan for my education model." All her industry experience convinced her that companies struggled for talent, even as they grew exponentially. "I felt it was the right time to revisit the education model I was familiar with and to do it in a different way and launch a new venture."

Training the Educated

The business plan for Global Talent Track took about 18 months to develop and fine-tune. Then, Uma started meeting with venture funds and explaining her model to them. When the funding was all tied up, the venture was launched.

Getting the right talent, at the right place and at the right price, is a tricky business. Industries and companies want people with a particular set of skills, at a particular cost. This formula is set and is difficult to deviate from. On the other hand, job aspirants are willing to get trained if they are assured a particular compensation. So the challenge lies in converging the needs of the two segments.

In developed and mature economies, the ecosystem is highly advanced. "In developed countries, it is possible for both ends to be planned. A particular industry would be growing at a certain rate and it needs so many engineers, workers and supervisors. They have a fairly mature training, educational and vocational system. And schools, universities, institutions, from where they source their employees. If they cannot meet their requirements from within the country, they import what they need from outside."

But in India, industry growth and opportunities have outstripped the availability of talent. "Education has not been dovetailed with the industry demands." A perfect example of this was in the '90s, when there was a sudden spike in the demand for computer professionals, and there was a mad rush to include Computer Engineering in the course curricula. "But did we ensure that we had enough quality teachers, PhDs, to teach the subject?"

Again in 2003-04, the industry clamoured for more engineers, and private engineering colleges and institutes mushroomed in every state. However, Uma says, not more than 60 percent of the seats in these engineering colleges are filled. To top that, because of the lack of quality teachers, of the one million-odd engineering students graduating every year, not more than 20-25 percent is readily employable.

There are three components to the talent-crunch problem — one, the engineers graduating are not meeting the industry's requirements. Two, there are engineering institutes in plenty but the seats are not getting filled up. Three, the government is saying that more people are needed.

So, the whole issue of employability and getting the right talent boils down to companies wanting people at a specific location, who are equipped with all the skill sets that a specific job entails, at a particular salary.

The job aspirants also need to be motivated to get trained or educated because they have to know what kind of a job they will be getting at the end of it.

The rural employment schemes like NREGA have actually

compounded the problem in one way. In those states where it is running successfully, people are reluctant to come to the urban areas to be employed, as they are getting paid to do work where no great skills are required. The only way in which these people can be induced to acquire skills and re-locate is to hold out the incentive of a higher salary.

Global Talent Track works on three aspects to raise the employability level of graduates — imparting communication skills relevant to a particular role, improving technical skills, and improving domain knowledge.

"We work very closely with state governments, colleges, universities, corporates, and small and medium enterprises, to understand the gaps in talent and train the workforce appropriately."

Various state governments have different employment agencies, with whom Global Talent works under specific mandates, to cover a district, college or domain to find the right people.

The average timeline for these engagements varies from 3 weeks to a year, depending on the area and the needs of the organisation.

"We look at people who are in the 60 to 70 percent range in terms of learning and then we try to bridge the gap. The challenge is how to take this learning up to 90 percent. The remaining 10 percent, they can learn on the job."

When working with corporates, Uma's company engages with them closely to find out their requirements. Once these are identified, they are broken down into disparate components — which can help them get the right skill sets and the training methodology to be used, and estimate the extent of training to be given.

Delivery of the training is also important as students' attention has to be engaged. "So we look at delivering content in the form of games, computer-based exercises and role-playing."

The main challenge that she faces in her enterprise is the surrounding infrastructure, which is not yet well-defined and is still evolving.

Agility and flexibility are important as the company has to be profitable too. "As the industry grows, their needs keep changing and we have to be alert and change our business models accordingly," she says.

"However, we hope to evolve the ecosystem as we go along."

Global Talent has now diversified to Malaysia and China. In Malaysia, the delivery is virtual and online, unlike that in India, where her team is physically present at the venues.

China is becoming an active competitor to India in the outsourcing arena in software services and there is a huge opportunity there, as the country is determined to give its people the right kind of skills to make them ready to be employed in the IT sector.

The company has also recently expanded its services to Jordan.

"We have got to see how we can bring in respect for ability and skills. Our goal is to be a life-long partner with the candidates, rather than just stopping at making them employable."

●

7

I AM BORN FOR GREATER THINGS

Renuka Ramnath

Founder and CEO
Multiples Alternate Asset Management

Renuka Ramnath, Founder and Chief Executive of private equity firm Multiples Alternate Asset Management, is one of few, refreshingly honest women, who makes no bones about the fact that the quest for money, financial security and a good position were the chief drivers that led her up the corporate ladder.

After spending 23 years in the ICICI Group, spending 8 of them as Head of what she built into the country's leading venture capital firm, ICICI Ventures, Renuka launched her own private equity firm in 2009, which has the backing of Indian banks, financial institutions and overseas investors, including pension funds.

"Yes, I was very ambitious. I wanted to make a lot of money. My sister tells me that I would say that I wanted to be the Managing Director of a company."

Renuka has realised both her ambitions. She became the Managing Director of ICICI Ventures in 2001, and now she is the boss of her own investment firm. As to a lot of money, she recently moved into a luxury apartment in a mid-town, high-rise building in Mumbai, buying the flat for Rs 8 crore.

Born to middle-class Tamil parents in Chembur, (a suburb in India's financial capital, Mumbai) Renuka, the middle of three children, was a willful and contrary child. She had to get her own way, and immediately.

At the age of three, seeing her cousins being taught Carnatic music, she wanted to learn it too. She was told that she would have to wait until she was five before she could learn. Renuka however did not want even a single day's delay and took to standing outside the room where the music lessons were being held and banging on the door. Her family finally relented and allowed her to join in.

Education and career were very important to her. She remembers being first in class and crying because she had scored just 10 marks more than the student who came in second. "I wanted to be 50, 60 marks ahead. It was important for me to lead by a wide margin."

"I saw education as a way to realise all my ambitions… Education was my anchor, my foundation."

Her interests were wide and varied, tending towards the fine arts — music, stitching, embroidery, *rangoli,* clay work and of course, her studies.

Renuka gives a lot of credit to her mother for the support and encouragement she gave the girls in the family. Since she herself didn't get an opportunity to go to college and make a career, she was determined that her two daughters should have every opportunity to achieve their aspirations.

"Hats off to my mother — for a person who's not been to college and grew up in a village, with zero exposure and a meek demeanour, she was determined that we should have the same opportunities as her son did, if we so desired."

The Textile Engineer

Renuka's degree in textile engineering came about by 'pure serendipity'. After finishing her higher secondary studies from SIES College, there was a lot of discussion in the family as to what was to be her next course of action.

Her father wanted her to be a doctor. Her grandmother was dead against the idea of her getting into the medical profession because her husband was an Ayurveda doctor, and she had developed a strong grouse against the profession based on the long and irregular hours he kept. "She prayed to all the Gods she knew so that I would not become a doctor," Renuka quips fondly.

Her good scores in Mathematics and her poor marks in Biology decided it for her. It was to be engineering.

Her brother, who was older than her, supported the engineering cause but did not want her to join Veermata Jijabai Technological Institute (VJTI) and recommended UDCT instead, which is now Mumbai University Institute of Chemical Technology.

His view was that VJTI was a male-dominated college, and as such, not really suitable for her. His specific injunction to her was — "If you apply to VJTI, I'll break your legs."

Renuka, you must remember, delighted in being contrary. So while she did apply to UDCT, she could not resist the temptation to cross the road to VJTI which stood on the opposite side, to try her luck there. As she wandered across the sprawling campus trying to locate the admissions office, a male student spotted this lone girl wandering about and asked her if he could help.

"I want to get an application form for admission," Renuka told him.

"Electrical? Mechanical, Civil? Or is it textiles?"

The word 'textile' struck Renuka as a heaven-sent inspiration. Maybe it was the electrical, mechanical and chemical engineering streams that her brother had warned her against. Those sounded like all-male subjects. Textiles sounded very feminine to her. He should have no problem with that. Thus reasoned Renuka.

"Textile engineering," Renuka said, upon which she was directed to the appropriate building. She put in her bid for the course, but after doing it she began to suffer from the reaction of going against an older brother's diktat.

She felt faint, nauseous and while returning home, got on the wrong bus as well. She reached home in a state of near-collapse and decided not to tell anyone about what she had done.

Textiles, she says, was much more competitive than any other stream because there were only 20 seats for the course. Most of the seats were reserved on some quota or the other, so there were only 5 seats actually available on merit. Renuka didn't make it in the first two lists, but her name was there on the third list. By that time, she had already joined as an undergraduate in SIES college.

She returned home from college one day to be greeted with joy by her mother who told her that she had got an interview call from VJTI. Renuka's immediate reaction was to tell her mother to throw the call letter into the bin.

"I am not going to attend the interview," she said.

"Don't be stupid," her mother admonished her. "VJTI is such a good college."

When her brother came to know of it, he said, "Do as you please. But don't say I didn't warn you."

Her mother accompanied Renuka to the interview. When they arrived at the college, the first thing they saw was a sea of blacks. VJTI had a reputation for its textile engineering course and since the textile sector was important for Africa, this college had a huge patronage from students there.

"Maybe we should go away," suggested her mother, intimidated by all this show of male brawn.

"No, of course not. I'll attend the interview," said Renuka stoutly, having quite made up her mind to study textile engineering now.

Her interview started on a discouraging note. The principal told her that VJTI being a government-run college, he could not deny her admission but that she could find it tough going since she would be the only girl in her batch.

She would have to attend training in a textile mill, and that would be an impossible task, because no textile mill would accept a girl in their workshop. After graduation, she would not be able to join anywhere because nobody would employ her. Maybe she should reconsider her candidature, the principal suggested.

Renuka was unmoved by that argument and joined VJTI.

It was just as the principal had predicted. It was tough. The boys did not speak to her and left her strictly alone. Many of them were from the smaller towns of Maharashtra, surrounding Mumbai, and as such not equipped to deal with a 'city girl.'

They were also apprehensive that if any of them approached her or spoke to her, they would be labelled her 'boyfriend' — something to be avoided at all costs.

The situation got so intolerable that it reduced Renuka to tears. There was a girl, a couple of years her senior, who sternly told Renuka to stop feeling sorry for herself and wallowing in her misery. "Crying will not help you."

After about six months of this, things started to change for the better. Academically, Renuka was still excelling. This predisposed some of the brighter boys in her favor. In the practical classes, she showed a lot of independence by operating the machines in the workshop on her own — a maneuver which occasioned no little merriment from her male colleagues, the first few times they saw her in action.

She persevered and gradually penetrated their reserve and hostility. By the end of the year, she had been accepted and fully integrated into their fellowship. She identified herself so much as one of the boys, that she also fell into the habit of whistling and making catcalls when encountering the stray girl on campus or in the corridors!

Towards the end of her course, there was an international seminar in India and the college had a team of visitors from Texas Women's University. Impressed at finding this solitary girl taking the textile course, they offered her a doctorate programme at the university, a chance Renuka jumped at because she wanted so much to go the US, and anyway, in India, no textile company was going to employ her.

Thrilled as always, it was her mother who made the rounds of the banks to get her the necessary guarantees and to take care of other paperwork which had to be done. Even as it looked like it was all settled and she would be going to Texas, her more conservative father put his veto on it.

"Whatever you want to study, you do it here itself in India. Otherwise, I'll get you married and then you can go to America." But Renuka did not want to get married just to go to the US.

It was too late by then to prepare for any of the major entrance exams for management courses, and so she took the entrance test for Bombay University's Masters in Management Studies course and joined Chetana's RK Institute of Management & Research.

At Chetana's, she discovered her aptitude for finance, and in the autumn of 1984, Renuka, armed with a Masters in Management, with finance as her specialisation, was ready to step into the corporate world.

Working Life
ICICI — The Wonder Years

Renuka Ramnath has been identified so strongly with the ICICI Group, many people believe that she started her career in the bank itself. However, during campus recruitment season at Chetana's, she was interviewed by Hindustan Unilever (which did not make an offer) and got offers from power equipment maker Crompton Greaves, and ICICI with whom she had done her summer internship.

She joined Crompton Greaves. Her explanation was — "I didn't want to start out in my career with a big brand like ICICI right away. It would have been too cushy a job."

She worked with Crompton Greaves for almost two years, and while she got a lot of insight into the world of manufacturing, and the myriad issues and challenges it presents, the work was not satisfying and eventually, she grew bored.

She applied to ICICI again, and joined it in 1986, as a Trainee Officer.

In the mid '80s, India's economy was still closed. ICICI was then the Industrial Credit and Investment Corporation of India, a development financial institution providing long-term project finance to infrastructure companies, and headed by the doyen of Indian financial services, Narayanan Vaghul.

ICICI put her first in the Merchant Banking division, which was not a big business for the company at the time. Investment banking, during those days, was not quite what it is now. There were no mergers and acquisitions worth the name happening nor were corporates queuing up to raise funds.

Around this time, Renuka got married and had her first child, and took it easy on the career front. However, when she came back from her maternity leave, she plunged into her work with a vengeance, eager to make up for lost time.

The merchant banking unit in ICICI consisted of two activities

— Corporate Finance and Public Issues. There was some slight action on the Public Issues front but Corporate Finance was practically non-existent. The business had to be grown. Renuka asked to be put in the Public Issues department but was told that she was hired as a resource for Corporate Finance. Some senior people from ICICI's Operations side were also transferred to the unit to boost that business.

"That was the best thing that happened to me," Renuka says of the time spent in Corporate Finance, where she worked till 1997. She was part of the team which had to go and win assignments, sign mandates and get fees. "One had to prove oneself by being capable enough to get the business."

Five years after she joined, the department was sold to US investment bank J P Morgan, under a joint venture agreement with ICICI. The team got a chance to go to New York and was exposed to global best practices in finance. "We were part of the J P Morgan global network."

After 1991, economic liberalisation brought in more projects and even more exposure for Renuka and the whole team. "With J P Morgan's expertise and our training, our confidence, the language that we spoke, the way we thought... everything changed."

This was the time when Renuka had her second child, a daughter, and she started to wonder whether she should take a sabbatical to look after her child, who was very dependent on her. It was also an emotional wrench for Renuka to leave her daughter behind every day to go to work.

She was ruminating on this when tragedy hit. Her husband — who had always encouraged her and supported her in her career and who was her emotional bulwark — died in a car crash in 1993.

All thoughts of a sabbatical fled. She had to provide emotional as well as financial security for her children.

"When my husband died, my immediate objective was that my children should see no pain. They should not see their mother cry." She wanted to ensure that they would not miss anything in life and would have the same holidays, education and comfort as before.

"That put a huge sense of purpose in my life." Her family rallied around her as did her colleagues at ICICI.

She did go through periodic self-doubt, because she had always relied on her husband for both professional and personal decisions. "I used to think of him as this all-pervading personality, who knows it all and can do it all. There was this huge question mark in my mind — can I do it alone?"

The ICICI-J P Morgan venture broke up in 1999, but a couple of years before that happened, she was whisked away by Shikha Sharma (the current head of Axis Bank) who co-opted her to join the Structured Finance group in ICICI.

The years spent in the Corporate Finance and Structured Finance groups gave her a good grounding in dealing with corporates and understanding their financing needs.

The Structured Finance business was also her first taste of working in a start-up environment, as this was a new initiative for ICICI. New-age companies going global were looking for more innovative methods of getting credit and finance for their expansion and diversification needs.

For Renuka, it was exciting to conceptualise a new business, to put together a new team, train them, go out and sell the products, get the credibility in the market and of course, make money for the group. "It was a phenomenal experience and turned out to be a successful business."

She was part of the Structured Finance group till 1999, and when she left, it contributed close to 40 percent of ICICI's incremental assets.

Straight after this, Renuka went to Harvard Business School where ICICI sponsored her to enroll in the Advanced Management Programme.

Renuka took the Harvard stint very seriously. She considered it a clean break in her career and made up her mind that she would not go back and do the same job. She worked very hard during the course, and as she says, "…allowed myself to be inspired by all the case studies." It instilled a lot of confidence in her and she was pleasantly surprised to find that many of her colleagues there — CEOs of global corporations — thought very highly of her.

"I returned with loads of confidence."

The dawn of a new century brought with it new beginnings. The last few years of the 20th century had seen new business opportunities emerging, and especially in the online space, entrepreneurship had suddenly become the watchword, as people with little or no experience began dreaming of becoming internet millionaires.

Sabeer Bhatia, who had founded the hugely popular Hotmail, was the poster boy of online success, after he sold the web-based mail service to Microsoft for a rumored $400 million in 1998. Anyone with a remotely saleable idea wanted to monetise it.

Terms such as 'angel investors' and 'venture capitalists', that were hitherto unknown in India, were now on everyone's lips. It was rumoured that these financiers were just waiting to write out cheques for a million dollars, at the very least, for your ideas.

Then in 2000, the dot com bust happened and the climate for entrepreneurial enterprise soured.

When Renuka, brimming with energy and confidence, returned from Harvard, K V Kamath, who had taken over as Chief Executive in 1996, put her in charge of the e-commerce business in ICICI, saying that it was more relevant for the group.

Renuka worked on the business like she was possessed. "I was oozing energy. I did so many things. I never went home. I worked seven days a week, 18 hours a day." She started the internet payment gateway system, the electronic bill payment company Bill Junction, and cafe portals. She made investments in a few technology firms and set up ICICI's intranet network. She even wanted to set up a global platform for e-enabling some banks in the United States.

"It was a maniacal period for me at that time. People in ICICI wondered what had happened to me."

The top management felt that since she was displaying such exemplary entrepreneurial abilities, she could be put in charge of the unit dealing with entrepreneurs.

"That was how I got there — ICICI Ventures — in January 2001."

Mother of Private Equity

Renuka had already won recognition within ICICI Bank for the energy and zeal that she displayed in her various roles within the bank, but ICICI Ventures gave her an identity of her own, and enormous recognition within the sector. She won her spurs in the venture unit, in a manner of speaking, and became a powerful force to reckon with, in the group's corporate hierarchy.

She built the unit from scratch, riding out the lows and stepping up the pace when the industry environment was conducive to growth. From a non-entity and marginal player in the segment, she transformed ICICI Ventures into the largest domestic venture firm in the industry, striking shrewd deals and making investments, banking on the experience that she had gathered in the Corporate and Structured Finance groups.

ICICI's star performer, however, had a less than impressive start in the venture capital industry. It was not quite what she had imagined. The period between 2001 and 2004 was one of the worst patches in her life proving to be a trial by fire for her, testing her patience, ingenuity and the ability to keep going despite lack of success.

It was a difficult environment to attract investors. Indian investors were eyeing any request for funds with suspicion, and overseas investors had burnt their figures with inflated valuations for ventures which were found to be not sustainable.

The early years of the century also saw a lot of uncertainty in the stock markets with the Ketan Parekh scam, and a series of other, smaller, financial irregularities surfaced, which impacted investor confidence. The climate of suspicion was aggravated by the September 2001 attacks on the World Trade Centre and the Pentagon in the US.

Without the backing of investors and funds, there was very little investing she could do.

"Those three years were hell for me. Professionally, this period was as bad for me as the death of my husband had been on a personal level," says Renuka.

Nothing was happening. She couldn't get money for her funds. The portfolio companies were too young, her team very inexperienced. ICICI, as the parent, did not give her any more money for the venture, asking her to raise the funds from external sources. "We'll just watch you," they told her.

As the chief of a very small subsidiary of a huge financial services company, she confessed to feeling "…very small. I would go and sit in these corporate meetings, where you find your peers representing much bigger businesses." She was not contributing to the profits of the group and the very existence of the venture came under question.

Kamath began to wonder if he had done the right thing in sending this dynamic resource to a non-performing unit. There were even talks about closing it down and bringing Renuka back to the bank.

But now it had become almost an ego issue with Renuka, who was determined that she would make a success of the venture somehow. "There was this great desire in me to make ICICI Ventures very relevant to ICICI." Conscious of the responsibility of a team looking up to her renewed her determination.

"Either I set the venture right or I leave the group."

She attributes her eventual success to the blessings of her spiritual guru (who told her not to give up), her hard work and the inherent doggedness in her character, which refused to admit defeat. "I have this characteristic within me, that no matter where you throw me, I'll eventually come out successful. I don't think uni-directionally. I'm always thinking of other ways and means to get a job done. I can reach out to people and motivate them to do the dirtiest job."

In early 2004, the Indian economy started to boom. Two major IPOs hit the market — one was Tata Consultancy Services, and next, the government divested stake in its richest undertaking, Oil and Natural Gas Corporation (ONGC).

Investor sentiment bounced back. New funds were registering themselves with the Securities and Exchange Board of India, hedge funds were investing in Indian equities in droves. And venture firms started to get investors.

This was just the opportunity that Renuka had been waiting for. With the economic environment working in her favor, she plunged herself into the task of re-building ICICI Ventures. It took her slightly over a year to set the legacy portfolio working, create a new best practices platform, raise funds and train and motivate her team with a vision to work for. She also negotiated with ICICI for a profit sharing arrangement with her portfolio companies.

Much like Zia Mody, who was called the Big Mama of corporate law, Renuka came to be known as the 'Mother of private equity'.

When she took over the firm, it had less than $50 million in third party funds. When she left in 2009, it was managing a corpus of over $2 billion. Apart from working out the most innovative deals, ICICI Ventures also made a neat profit of Rs 1500 crore for the bank that year.

ICICI Ventures is credited with handling the first management buyout, the first structured finance deal, the first mezzanine fund, the first real estate fund. Besides buying large stakes in unlisted companies.

The first company it invested in was multiplex firm PVR Ltd for Rs 38 crore. The largest deal it entered into was with Dr Reddy's in 2005, when the companies announced a $56 million partnership for the commercialisation of Abbreviated New Drug Applications to be filed over two years.

In its second fund, ICICI Ventures raised about $800 million. The company was setting up a chain of hospitals through a health-care fund I-Ven Medicare, a part of its India Advantage Fund.

"I had nurtured a fantastic team and we had a great working environment. It was an unimaginable run I had. Eight years went off like eight minutes."

Becoming her Own Boss

Then came the Subhiksha debacle in 2008. ICICI Ventures had a 33 percent stake in the Chennai-based retail chain that ran into cash problems and ultimately had to suspend operations. Renuka's venture firm sold off about 10 percent in the company to Azim Premji's personal investment arm, Zash Investment, for about Rs 230 crore, just a few months prior to its shutting operations.

Subhiksha was a big blot on an otherwise impeccable track record.

In hindsight, Renuka admits that the monitoring of the investment in Subhiksha should have been more disciplined. "Subhiksha was a great learning experience for me in starting Multiples. Now I will find it difficult to place unquestioned trust in anybody. We learnt many lessons from it."

They dealt with Subhiksha's founder R Subramanian in a low-key manner. When his problems surfaced, ICICI Ventures gave him the benefit of the doubt because of his background and the kind of company he was trying to set up.

"But we did not put our foot down and tell him — 'If you have not done this, I will not let you do that.'"

When they suggested that he follow a certain course of action, his reply was that he knew he had to do it but then he had a thousand other things to do as well.

Renuka makes sure that she doesn't repeat the same mistake now with Multiples. "So now I will tell my entrepreneurs — you will have to do this and that. If you cannot do it, don't run the show. Until you cannot get the back-end right, I will not let you go ahead with the front-end roll-out."

She has also learnt the value of keeping all records of transactions, maintaining the paperwork, getting timely information, being firm with the promoters and taking immediate action. "This has been a great preparation for me in setting up Multiples."

Subhiksha left a bad taste in the mouth — though nobody in ICICI really blamed her for it because of the grim realisation that investments going bad was something that could happen to anyone, considering the vagaries of the economic climate, and a promoter's temperament. However, what hurt Renuka was that nobody in ICICI came forward to help her.

In 2009, the leadership in ICICI was changing guard and Renuka ran into some conflict when she demanded more support from the parent for her pet venture, to keep it running profitably. The parent bank was not willing to fall in with her wishes. Her investors sided with her and it turned into an ugly confrontation between her and the bank. Renuka came to the realisation that she would have to leave the organisation where she had spent the greater part of her life, where she had so painstakingly built her reputation.

She does have some regrets about the way her exit from the

company was mismanaged, but she also sees it as a blessing, since it gave her the courage to venture out on her own. She spent some terrible months prior to her exit — "I thought I would die. I was going through emotional trauma and I had palpitations."

But the day she walked out of ICICI for the final time, she felt liberated and happy.

The transition from a high-flying corporate honcho to founding a start-up was another life-defining experience for Renuka — almost on par with setting up ICICI Ventures. "Once I left ICICI, there was no looking back for me. I have realised that you can give your heart and soul to an organisation, but in a large organisation, the day you quit, you are on the other side of the table and they treat you like an enemy."

"Actually ICICI has ceased to bother me. It doesn't evoke any emotion or response anymore. It looks like another life. I had a blast, I cut my teeth there, I built my reputation there, but now it's time to move on. This is a new life — a very logical, lovely transition."

After she left ICICI, and thought of setting up her own venture, she envisioned that it would take her a while convincing people to invest in her company, but the mammoth brand equity she had built up in ICICI Ventures paid off. Investors were more than willing to invest in her venture, and she also got offers from a couple of industrial houses to manage their own investment firms.

"I thought I would have to work very hard to convince investors, but to my surprise, the whole world was willing to meet and give me money."

Prospective investors told her, "You don't have to tell us your story. Just tell us if you have a company and you want to raise money." Consultancy firm KPMG even did her documentation for a token one rupee.

She managed to get Indian investors interested in her within six months of her quitting ICICI, the overseas investors taking a little more time due to their stringent processes.

Multiples has a dual structure, with the domestic side of her fund being backed by Indian banks such as Andhra Bank, Indian Overseas Bank, Punjab National Bank and insurance behemoth Life Insurance Corporation. On the international side, her investors are Commonwealth Development and Canada Pension Plan Investment Board, which committed funds up to $100 million.

Multiples aims to invest in mid-sized Indian companies across sectors, providing long-term investments, as well as to build companies from scratch, for entrepreneurs who have a sound and feasible business model. Leveraging on her vast experience with ICICI Ventures, her company also plans to be involved in management buyouts and funding of entities spun-off from large Indian groups.

Soon after she set up the company, she raised about $250 million from her investors in early 2010, and the size of her current fund has a cap of $450 million.

In early April this year, Multiples bought about 14 percent stake in Indian Energy Exchange, the country's largest power trading exchange firm, for about $14 million. At present, the independently-led private equity firm expects to make investments ranging from about $10 million to $50 million in individual firms.

So does work still obsess her? "Earlier I used to be obsessive about work. Now I am more relaxed. I am building up this venture with a lot of love... and slowly."

"If I had remained in ICICI, I would have been thinking of retirement in another eight years... and then what?"

After the frenetic pace of her earlier decades, she now believes in doing less and not making mistakes. She is also careful about whom she does business with. "Just because somebody is a big group doesn't make them good people."

The journey of Multiples so far, she says, has been extremely smooth and step-by-step. "I want to keep it that way."

She has a team of 25 people working with her in Multiples, including Sudhir Variyar as Investment Director (formerly Senior Director, ICICI Ventures), Prakash Nene as MD & CFO (formerly Group Director, Bharti Enterprises) and Nithya Easwaran as Investment Principal (Head of Structured Finance and Private Financing, Citibank, Mumbai).

Renuka does make it a point to appoint women in her company at all levels, and currently there are about seven women working for her — a fairly large proportion by private equity standards.

Renuka Ramnath's dream is to make Multiples a reputed, respected, aspirational institution, where a lot of professionals can come and realise their dreams — much like she achieved her own dreams at ICICI.

"I want to build a lot of successful enterprises and entrepreneurs, and I want to be the trusted bridge for bringing in a lot of international capital in India."

She knows it will be a long haul but she's mentally prepared for it. "It's not going to happen overnight. So I'm not even pushing the organisation to make anything happen overnight."

"Whatever we do, we'll do it perfectly. And one day, it'll happen."

●

8

A MISSION FOR EQUITY

Shaheen Mistri

Founder
Akansha and Teach for India

It is rather rare for a young girl to contemplate her vocation very early in life, and rarer still, to find it in working with children — how many 12-year olds do we know who spend summer vacations voluntarily working with disadvantaged children? How many teenaged girls would we find, willingly working in an orphanage during holidays, and helping speech and hearing-impaired children?

Shaheen Mistri, Founder of Akansha and Teach for India, was drawn towards children and animals at a very early age. Painfully shy as a child, she was in her element and at absolute ease with animals. The houses she lived in were always filled with stray animals she picked up from the streets to tend to them.

Born in an affluent Parsi family in Mumbai, Shaheen lived the first 17 years of her life globetrotting with her family, leading the comfortable, but rather rootless existence of an expatriate family, being educated in some of the best schools and growing up without a care in the world, cocooned in her privileged existence.

Her mother was a speech therapist and Shaheen was used to seeing speech and hearing-impaired children at their house, but this was her first, individual contact with the problematic world of differently abled children. The existence of another, darker world, beyond her ken, thrust itself into her consciousness. It unsettled her.

She translated her compassion for children into practical action and began spending her holidays and vacations engaging with them. During her visits to India, she worked with physically challenged children in an orphanage. While living in Indonesia, she worked in a home for autistic children.

Her grandmother, on her mother's side, was a strong influence on Shaheen during her growing up years. A rebellious woman, she lived life on her own terms and did exactly what she wanted to do, a quality which may have unconsciously rubbed off on Shaheen, when she decided to eschew a conventional career to follow the diktats of her heart.

It did not take Shaheen long to decide what she wanted to do in life, to determine what her priorities were. She did not have the usual struggle that teenagers and adolescents go through, wondering what to do with their lives. It happened to her 'organically' — since it meant transmuting her passion into her career, so to speak.

As she grew up and began to appreciate the enormity of the problems of inequity in the world, she knew she had to do something about it and that she had to make a difference. The stark contrast between her own childhood and that of the children she met in orphanages troubled her — the unfairness of it all and the inequitable distribution of wealth and opportunities made a lasting impression on her.

Shaheen and her brother had been brought up with the ability and freedom to make their own choices. But when Shaheen expressed a desire at the age of 18, to come to India for good, it was not an idea that her parents approved of immediately. Like any other parents, they wanted their daughter to go to university and get a job. However, when they saw her determination, despite their reservations, they allowed her to pursue her chosen path.

In the early '80s, it was not the norm for expatriate Indians to return to India, which was still a closed economy with very few career opportunities outside the traditional streams of engineering and medicine. If you were lucky enough, you went out (of the country) and stayed out. Those with a brilliant education and those with the requisite purse strings, were all in pursuit of the American dream, en route to a kind of lifestyle that they could never aspire to in India.

The itinerant lifestyle which Shaheen and her family had, gave rise to a feeling of rootlessness — a sentiment that many of the first generation emigrant families of Indians struggled with. While they had settled in the US and UK to make a better life for their families and children, they carried within themselves the seeds of their Indian culture and upbringing that they clung to tenaciously, and which clashed with the alien customs of their adopted countries.

Shaheen felt this even more while staying in New York — she couldn't articulate that feeling but she had a sense of something missing in her life. She felt like an alien without any land to call home. As she grew older and as this feeling grew more intense, she decided that she wanted to explore her Indian roots. She was Indian but she had no real idea about the country of her birth.

She wanted to understand it. That was one motivation for her to return to India.

But a more compelling force was the drive to work with under-privileged children in India and to do something to alleviate the pathetic conditions that they were living in.

Discovering India — and Poverty

Shaheen's first concern after returning to India was to get into college, which she did, and opted to study sociology, the nearest thing to education she could find. Her early work with children in India had taught her that education was the key to turning around people's lives and giving them a new direction and purpose.

It was a clear and simple idea she had — give people the skills to think critically and then they would be able to make their own decisions. She also felt that sociology was a subject that could give her an insight into India and help her understand the issues and challenges that the country was labouring under. Later, she did her Masters in Education from Manchester University, United Kingdom.

Shaheen's initial work with children from the slums in Mumbai was not so much about education as it was about giving them a space where they could be safe and indulge in activities designed to take away the grimness of their lives.

"It was as simple as that. I think I was constantly comparing the children I came into contact with, with my own childhood… and I felt it just wasn't fair. The idea of equity became a huge part of my life right in the beginning."

Many questions plagued her, to which she had no answers. Why was it that she had opportunities while children of a particu-lar community didn't? Why did they have to look after younger siblings at a tender age, while she grew up without a care in the world?

"So, more than kids and education it was about how something in this world is wrong and unfair. That was what drew me to this work."

The biggest advantage that really worked in her favour was her total devotion to children and the fact that she loved spending every minute of her time with them. "That was something that I got my greatest energy from and I still do. I just love to be with kids and the feeling that I get when I am able to connect with them — to me, it's a feeling like no other I have ever experienced."

She did not stop to think and logically chart out her course of action. She just walked into a slum in Cuffe Parade in Mumbai and made friends with a girl, of about her own age, but from as different a background from her own as it was possible to find. Shaheen didn't know the local language and the girl, Sandhya, didn't know English but the two connected at a deeper level and got on very well together.

She also managed to get an introduction to a senior reporter from *The Times of India* and got permission to accompany him on his news rounds. This enabled her to visit places that she would have otherwise found hard to gain access to — courts, prisons, police stations — the seamier side of Mumbai, so to say.

Shaheen's friendship with Sandhya, whom she visited every day after college, exposed her to a way of life that was, to her, unimaginable. How could people live with so little? It removed many of the misconceptions that she had about poverty.

It was at Sandhya's house that she first started teaching the slum children who dropped by. "I started teaching them a little bit of English. Her house became the classroom and that's how it all started."

The first year that she spent working in the slum was an eye-opener for her. "That was the phase that really shook me up, in terms of my commitment to equity."

She witnessed things which she found unacceptable — a

woman burned to death; a child in flames; a baby dying due to dehydration. "There was this woman from Karnataka who had seven children and she couldn't understand why she was producing so many of them. I spoke to her about birth control — it turned out that the husband had been taking the birth control pills and not the wife." The utter ignorance and pathos of the lives of people in the slums, and their callousness towards life, stunned her.

The enduring and hard, practical lessons in reality that Shaheen learned during this period shaped the course and goals of her life. She and a few of her college friends would all meet to discuss the ways that they could make education an enjoyable experience for the children, so that they could benefit more from it. They drew from their own experiences in their schools and what they had loved about their schools the most.

At the core of it all was the idea that children should have fun while learning. The processes were not so important as the results. Making learning relevant to the children, delivering it to them in an interactive format — these were common-sense ideas and these still hold good at the core of Shaheen's ventures today. "I didn't go out of my way to study exactly how it was to be done, and then take all that theoretical knowledge and apply it. I just learned along the way and I'm happy it happened the way it did."

It was not all easy. While the children were interested in getting educated, capturing and retaining their attention was a task in itself. The parents too, were initially hostile and indifferent to her efforts. They had had experiences in the past with social workers who approached them and made promises which never fructified. They also found it difficult to take this young girl — who looked strange and had a stranger accent — seriously.

It took her a while to get past that barrier of instinctive mistrust the slum-dwellers felt towards anything foreign, and build a relationship of trust with them. "When they saw that I was here to stay and was not going to give up on their kids, when they saw that more people from our side were coming in, they began to trust us." They were also skeptical about what all this education would do to their children and whether it would benefit them in any way.

The process of teaching and getting more involved with their education and lives also triggered off a process of change in her, sharpening her focus and objectives. While previously, she would ask herself, 'What do I want to do,' she now began asking, 'Where am I needed the most' and 'Where can I create the maximum change'.

Akansha — A New Hope

During the early days of Shaheen's involvement with children in the slums of Mumbai, she had no thoughts of forming an organisation or a society. So long as she was teaching the children within the slum itself, it worked fine. Then it occurred to her that the children should have a chance to feel what it would be like to learn in a real school environment.

She hunted for a suitable place and after much effort — this was Mumbai, after all, where land always comes at a premium — she found a space in Colaba which met her requirements and set up her first centre there.

Then she realised that the children had to be transported out of the slums, which meant hiring a bus; so there were costs involved in running the school now and that meant formalising her venture. And Akansha was established in 1991.

"When I say established, all of us were college students — there were seven of us. We formed the initial board of trustees."

The Akansha Foundation is all about providing education to children from slums and low-income households. It started out by providing non-formal education or what was called as after-schools. English, Math and values were what was mainly taught in these after-schools.

The challenges were many. Winning over the parents of the children was only a small step in the process. Making the children understand was the next step. They had to be told that the world was not a fair place and that theirs was a deprived existence. Their lives were tough and they would have to work very hard to make a success of their lives. Shaheen and her team could empathise with their plight but could not pity them as that would defeat their very purpose of making them self reliant and would merely perpetuate their current way of life.

It was a tough balancing act that the founding members of Akansha had to tread — being kind to the children while equipping them to become successful, independent individuals.

Shaheen and the founding members spent many years as teachers. The small group raised money through donations from family, friends and others. Shaheen's father worked in Citibank, and his colleagues and friends, who saw that this girl was doing something very different from what their own children were pursuing, pitched in with money.

Every sum of money received was very vital to the fledgling organisation that Shaheen and her band of friends were building.

"When we started having more centres, we started a scheme called 'Sponsor a school' whereby donors could adopt particular centres. That worked pretty well and kept the costs low."

When they wanted to scale up their operations and needed more funds, they began approaching corporates. For many years, Akansha did not have any problems getting funds. Education was something that everyone recognised and appreciated the need for. It was not a story that needed to be sold, since it was an established fact that one of the primary ways that poverty could be reduced in India was through education. And people and organisations were more than anxious to do their bit.

"We were working with volunteers. A lot of people were coming into our centres and supporting us. People who were sponsoring our centres tended to make multi-year commitments to the children."

"Everybody understands that children deserve equal opportunities. I've always felt that my job is a lot easier than many other non-profits that are really trying to fight for much more niche causes and things that don't really apply to everybody. In our case, if you are privileged and you see the opportunities that your children get and someone talks to you about giving and extending those opportunities to those less fortunate, it is very hard to say 'no.'"

Shaheen's naivete and touching belief in the underlying goodness of people and an ability to see the best in them also ensured that she met with very little opposition in her efforts. "Being young and being a woman — the combination worked. And since I had come from abroad, it made an interesting story. People liked to listen and seemed to want to help."

"I've always felt that the help we've got through the years and even today has very little to do with me and everything to do with the idea of the work and my ability to present it. Obviously though, communication is key."

Shaheen and Akansha were overwhelmed by the support they received. Often, there are many preconceived notions and biases operating in the minds of people, especially when they think about government organisations and corporates. A widely prevalent notion is that people in the government are notoriously slow when it comes to decision-making or extending support in any way. Corporates are imagined to be hard nuts to crack when it comes to charitable acts.

However, within these stereotypes, Shaheen was pleasantly surprised to find pockets of people who went out of their way to help her. For her, it was just a matter of finding the people who shared the same ideology as her.

The biggest support she received in terms of work was from the student community. When she reached out to students from St. Xavier's to rope them in as teaching volunteers, she was amazed at the response she got from them. She sat in the college canteen and posed the question to them — "Do you think you can make a difference in India, do you want to make a difference?" An overwhelming majority admitted that they were interested and willing to make a difference but they did not know how to go about it.

"They just need a platform and someone to take that first step with them."

Shaheen saw herself as a facilitator, as the provider of a platform where those who were needy could find a meeting ground with those who had the resources to give.

"We had the resources — the minds of kids we had to work with, they wanted to be educated; the college students who are fantastic resources of teaching; schools; spaces; funding. All we needed to do was bring these together and give people the ability to give. They (people) want to give, they just don't know how to make a difference."

Akansha — which had its genesis in a shanty in a Mumbai slum — now teaches about 4,000 children across its after-schools and traditional school models. The after-schools provide extra education to children who are already enrolled in government schools. In the last few years, Akansha has also moved into the regular school set-up where it is partnering with the local state government to independently run its own schools. There are 22 after-schools and 13 government schools between Mumbai and Pune. Anu Aga of Thermax, who is on the board of Akansha, has been responsible for taking the Akansha initiative to Pune.

The government schools are staffed by teachers recruited by Akansha, the motive being to maintain the standards of teaching in these schools. "We ensure quality of teaching because the accountability lies with Akansha. We have very intensive training support and multiple systems in place to ensure that quality is maintained."

Shaheen's endeavour is now to introduce the US charter school model in India. In the US, charter schools were started when parents were not satisfied with the education system in traditional public schools or found them too restrictive. Charter schools are run by money from organisations, individuals or the government, but may not be subject to the same rules that govern regular channels of education. Under Shaheen's model, people would be encouraged to come and work in communities that have the highest poverty levels, and run schools independently — but in close collaboration with the government.

"Akansha is trying to see a similar movement in India. Anyone who can turn around a government school and add value should be able to come in and enter into a contract with the government, whereby they are held accountable for student learning. Today nobody believes that government schools can be run differently with the same money."

Any kind of reform in India takes place at a snail's pace, since it means adjusting to and working with an entirely new set of parameters. Organisations such as Akansha see themselves as the agents of change who can influence policy making at the highest levels and induce reforms to take shape where they matter the most.

Shaheen is no longer operationally involved with the running of Akansha, but as Founder and Chairperson, she is in dialogue with the government to initiate reforms in the education sector, at the primary and secondary levels. "The government is in the process of passing legislation that will allow it to pay more for this kind of initiative to fructify. Say, you were to run a government school, then the government would bear 50 to 70 percent of the cost of running the school. It is a scalable model and more people can do it and they can be involved with multiple schools."

When that happens, Shaheen feels that it will be a sustainable way of imparting education and taking it forward. "The government is very responsive to this and they are trying to do a lot in their schools. It's obviously a long process of discussion, and very sensitive, because you have to be careful to ensure that no one tries to manipulate the system."

The Second Innings — Teach for India

For 17 years, Shaheen lived and breathed Akansha, which grew and expanded under her light touch. Along the way, Shaheen got married, but it was a short-lived union, which broke up when she was just six months' pregnant with her first child.

It was difficult bringing up a child on her own and as a single mother, while devoting herself to her all-consuming passion: the education of under-privileged children.

Her parents, whom she had left behind in America when she returned to India, had also decided to join her, and it was with their support and help that she brought up her children. When her elder daughter was about five years old, she adopted a baby girl.

"Bringing up my girl all alone was not easy. I was lucky — five years after I returned to India, my parents relocated to Mumbai. There's no way I would have been able to do what I did, without them. My parents have been absolutely amazing in the kind of support they have given me."

As is usual in such situations, Shaheen felt a lot of guilt, since her dedication to the work left her with very little time to spend with her children. There were no weekends free to spend with them. "But now I don't feel guilt at all. I don't bother about what other people tell me that my kids should have; I listen to myself and do what I feel my kids need. I really feel that I should set the example to my children — that here is a person who lives her life to her maximum potential."

Shaheen has lived her life according to that principle. She refused to get merely caught up in the roles that society deems it fit to thrust upon people — roles of a mother, daughter and wife. Inspired by her feisty grandmother — who had revelled in living life on her own terms — Shaheen feels that God gave her this one life and it was up to her to meet her potential and not live life according to someone else's expectations.

"I don't want that for my kids. Whatever they end up doing, I want them to feel that the biggest and foremost role in life is to live their potential. I think, that's the legacy I'll leave. To me, that's most important. Yes, there have been trade-offs — I'm not there to take them to every birthday party, I travel a lot and I'm not there all the time for a lot of the special things they need me for."

Even as she was building up Akansha and seeing the effect that education was having on the children, on their lives and their way of thinking, it struck her that there needed to be a systemic change — a change in the mindsets of the people who were in a position to take decisions. Akansha dealt with problems at the ground level in imparting education, but was it enough to bring about the change she envisaged? What if she could create a generation of leaders whose very reason for existence and whose whole belief system was bound up in obliterating these problems.

"I began to be fascinated by the idea of leadership, because I think the problem is that leaders across sectors in our country don't really care about equity for kids — if they did, the problem wouldn't exist."

What she needed to do was change the leaders and create the next generation of leaders who cared about this problem, and were skilled and committed to solving the problem.

"That's what led to the creation of Teach for India."

It was modeled on the Teach for America format, which had

been started in the US about 20 years ago.

Shaheen reasoned that the bright young talent in India usually opted to get into engineering or management studies and it was really the bottom 10 or 20 percent that went into the teaching profession. But if she had to harness these bright minds, she had to offer them sufficient options and incentives for them to take up the vocation of teaching. There had to be a platform for them.

Teach for India was the platform she envisaged and launched in 2008, to create a line of leaders in the country. Around this time, she could actually see the seeds of Akansha bearing fruit. The children she had taught so many years ago were getting into colleges, landing jobs and doing well for themselves. Children were still her passion, but she knew she had another mission.

Akansha would be fine without her. She had to let go. She didn't really plan to be away for a long time. Just enough to set up the new platform, put everything in place, get it running, stabilise it, and then she would get back to Akansha.

She got involved in the planning process, working with global consultancy firm McKinsey, to prepare a detailed blueprint. "At the end of it, we all looked around and said, "Okay, we now have a great new plan, we know it's feasible, we know it's inevitable and it's going to happen. But who's going to do it?"

They needed a full-time person to run the venture. Everybody declined, citing other commitments. Shaheen herself had her hands full with Akansha. By consensus, it was decided that she would run it until they could find another suitable candidate for the job. It took nearly a year for them to realise that there was no one else more suitable than her.

She officially became the CEO of Teach for India.

"So that's how it happened. Once I got into it, there was no going back. After the end of a year, when I saw our first batch and when I saw how in another 10 years, these people were going to be in positions of influence and they were going to be making a difference — there was no question of leaving it."

The Teach for India website gives a compelling description of what it aspires to do:

Teach for India recruits the most outstanding college graduates and young professionals to teach in low income, government and private schools for two years. Applicants go through a rigorous selection process where they are evaluated on academic excellence, demonstrated leadership, commitment to the community, critical thinking and perseverance, among other competencies.

Prior to and during the two-year Fellowship, Teach For India provides Fellows with the technical and leadership training required to achieve the goals they have set for themselves and their students.

Fellows are placed for two years as full time teachers in under-resourced schools in one of Teach for India's placement cities. They build relationships and have an impact beyond the classroom in the school and the community in which they are placed.

When it started out, the organisation had 87 Fellows, and so far, 827 Fellows have been part of the programme, in the four years of its existence. In 2009, it produced its first cohort of Fellows.

Unlike Akansha, which is pretty much a self-sustaining model, Teach for India is capital intensive, since the outfit is taking the best and brightest minds in the country and putting them to work. Also, it would work only if it could expand rapidly.

"When we went into it, we knew it would work only if we could scale it fast. There were so many areas we needed to impact — curriculum, teacher training, corporate social responsibility and so on. When you think of all the places they (the Fellows and as such future leaders of the country) need to go to, you know you need thousands of them out there to get into these positions. So we have tried to double our growth every year since we started."

Her vision and focus is to have 2,000 fellows in the programme in the next five years. "This means 1,000 alumni going into the workforce every year. It's a big task."

Teach for India is still dependent on donations for its survival but Shaheen hopes to attract big funds especially from the government, with whom she is in constant dialogue. Nita Ambani, wife of industralist and Chairman of Reliance Industries Mukesh Ambani, is on the board of Teach for India. Anu Aga is the Chairperson of the organisation.

"My belief is that good work is always sustainable and we need to improve and impact constantly. Every time I go into a meeting with the government or corporates and I find them to be non-responsive or unable to understand what we are doing, I think only one thing now — 'Oh my God! If only these people had been Teach for India fellows, the whole conversation would have been fundamentally different.'"

An Overwhelming Responsibility

Shaheen's fear when she started Teach for India was whether she was equipped to take on the responsibility of communicating her passion and driving force to the people whom she was recruiting and building to be the game changers.

She was a person who felt things deeply and her own personal life had its ups and downs — with the down phases being particularly energy-sapping experiences for her. Did she have it in her to sustain the levels of energy and passion, so that it could be a motivating and guiding force for the rest of them who were executing her dreams?

"This job profile requires me to have a lot of happiness and love within myself to be able to do this work properly. There have been times when I've gone through emotional and personal hardships where I questioned whether I have the necessary qualities to see it through.

"There are so many people who depend on me for their work — it's overwhelming, that responsibility.

"It's about taking India's best, most talented and idealistic people into this programme — if they don't have a good experience, we could turn that idealism into cynicism. I was very frightened of that, because, you must realise, these people could have done anything for the country but they'd chosen to come into education and participate in this initiative. It's still overwhelming."

Shaheen feels a deep empathy towards the people working in and associated with both her organisations, whether it is the children she is educating, the people she is grooming to take over as future change leaders in India, or those managing the activities. That intense bond she develops with people allows her the right to expect a lot from them in terms of their commitment to their work.

"I care very deeply about the people I work with. I love them, I really adore them. I know about their family lives and they become my best friends. I hold them very close to my heart."

"So I'm able to push them and push them really hard because I believe that excellence can come only when all of us push ourselves hard. And I set the bar very high; I'm demanding but in a very humane way."

"Anu (Aga) told me a long time ago that you have to show your humane face to people, because you are not superhuman, there's a part of you which is ordinary. That's helped me a lot as I want to be perceived as a humane leader."

Shaheen is also very idealistic and a dreamer, which has allowed her to view life in a more simplistic manner. "I make the world into a bit of a fairytale in my head. It makes life easier to live and it allows you to do a lot more than being practical does."

She sees herself being associated with Teach for India for another five years at least, until her goal of 2,000 fellows is achieved — or at least until she has the next big idea or vision for transforming India.

There are challenges ahead. Funding is a challenge as is working with the government and getting the right kind of people. Teach for India is growing at a rapid pace, and getting outstanding human capital who can sustain that growth is a challenge. Maintaining the core values and quality as the organisation goes pan-India is a big challenge.

Her work with the government on education of teachers is absorbing her more these days and she sees an active role for herself in policies related to education for children, as also in revamping the primary school education scenario in the country.

"I want to have a deeper understanding of the needs of children across the country and I want to start moving into geographical areas that are more difficult. Right now, we are in the metro cities — I want to push this programme into states like Bihar and Uttaranchal, in the next five years. I'll be pushing the realms of possibility as to where Teach for India can go.

●

9

AN IRON FIST IN A VELVET GLOVE

Anu Aga & Meher Pudumjee

Director and Chairperson
Thermax

The travails of her life sit rather lightly on recently nominated Rajya Sabha Member Anu Aga's shoulders, rather she carries her load very lightly, and she has not allowed her struggles to become the burden of her life.

She retains a child-like innocence, which is instantly refreshing. She is spontaneous, speaks from the heart and is passionate about giving back to society, to make it a slightly better world for the underprivileged.

As she says, she is much busier now with her social service activities, than when she was at the helm of affairs in boiler and heater maker Thermax.

Underneath that deceptive softness however, is a woman of steel and determination, a testimony to which would be the ruthlessness with which she dealt with an incompetent management in the year 2000, and brought Thermax back from the brink of collapse, from a time when the company's share prices had dipped to an all-time low, to the billion dollar company that it is today.

Anu retired from active involvement in Thermax about eight years ago, after passing on the baton of leadership to her daughter Meher Pudumjee. She is now a Director on the board of Thermax and has an office in the company's main office in Pune. She uses it mainly to oversee and administer the numerous social causes that she is involved with.

Her daughter Meher Pudumjee, who is now heading Thermax in a non-executive capacity, comes across as more deliberate and reflective, with a tendency to weigh her words before she speaks. "Mum is more visionary — looking down from 30,000 feet, more from the heart, more from the gut. But I'm the kind of person who likes to get into details. I like to find out about things and I like to do my homework before I get into something that's new. So I'm probably more head than heart."

There is no particular desire in both women that the company's succession plan in terms of management should include anyone from the family. So long as the company is managed properly in accordance with their high standards of ethics, taking its obligations towards reducing environmental pollution seriously, growing briskly and providing a good livelihood to the people employed in it, and so long as it is involved in corporate social responsibility (which both Anu and Meher are very passionate about), the two women are fairly satisfied with the status quo.

As Chairperson of the company built by her grandfather and father, Meher is very sure that her children will be the owners, as majority shareholders of the company, though she has no idea whether they will join the company, work in it or take on an executive and active role.

"My children are too young now. The company will go to the family because the shares are ours — so in that sense my children have every right to the shareholding." The family and the promoter group hold close to 62 percent stake in the company.

"It's like a trusteeship. We are the trustees of the company," says Meher.

However, whether the children would be in managerial or executive positions would depend entirely on them. The children would have to start work at the bottom as trainees, and work their way up, if they prove capable. "Let's face it — we have got all our wealth only in Thermax. So we want the best person to run the company. And the best person need not necessarily be from the family."

"But I'll never rule out the option of my children joining the company in an executive capacity," she says.

With the running of the company resting in the hands of professionals, both mother and daughter are now free to pursue (as far as feasible) their own interests. For Anu, it is the social work she is involved with — she plays an active role at Akanksha, a non-profit organisation which imparts education to slum children, and she is on the board of Teach for India, another educational initiative. She is also a member of the government's National Advisory Council.

Most of all, however, Anu likes to spend time with her grandchildren.

Meher is involved in putting in place systems which will enable Thermax to be a worker-friendly place, and she dreams of Thermax becoming a global leader in providing non-polluting energy management and conservation systems. Apart from running the company, she is also pursuing her passion for music — she is part of the Chamber Singers Choir in Pune, which she attends religiously every Tuesday.

With a presence in 75 countries across the world in Asia Pacific, Africa and the Middle East, CIS countries, Europe, USA and South America, 19 international offices, 12 sales & service offices and 4 manufacturing facilities — 3 of which are in India and one in China — Thermax has a significant presence in the boiler segment and air pollution control equipment industry.

At Thermax, it being a manufacturing company, the representation of women is low at 7 percent. This is because there are few women engineers passing out of institutes, and those who do, opt to go into software or get a management degree. Manufacturing is a low priority career choice for women engineers.

Thermax is now attempting to correct the imbalance by joining hands with certain engineering colleges, encouraging women to intern with them, so that they would have some idea about it and may be induced to join the company after graduation.

Its global technology partners include US-based Babcock & Wilcox, Japan's Kawasaki Thermal Engineering, Germany's Balcke, Durr and Lambion, and Canada's Eco-Tech.

A couple of years ago, it entered into an equity joint venture with Babcock & Wilcox Power Generation to manufacture supercritical boilers, which would have catapulted the company into another league. The project has been delayed due to various reasons but is expected to go on stream later this year. It also acquired European boiler maker Danstoker in the same year.

Shares of Thermax, which went public in 1995, are now trading at 450-levels. But this was not always so. There was a time in the late '90s when the company's share price had dipped to an alarming low and the two women, who were managing the company, found themselves in a quandary as to what they could do about it to bring it back on track.

Both Anu and Meher come across as anachronisms in the current cut-throat world of ambitious women in business. That they have been successful and built a successful company is a tribute to their understated managerial capabilities and should put to rest the myth that successful business women are necessarily aggressive and abrasive by nature.

Circumstances so arranged themselves as to thrust the two laid-back women into public glare and indeed propelled them into taking on leadership roles in the company.

Anu

Anu was born in an upper middle-class Parsi family, in Mumbai. Her father was very keen that his first-born should be a son. In fact, so keen was he on having a boy child that he remarked, probably in jest, "If the first child is a girl, I'll throw her out of the window." Anu was the third child and though a great favourite with her father, she says it looked like her acceptance was conditional.

The fact that she was a girl and hence unlike her brothers seems to have been reinforced at every point by her parents. Her brothers learned the violin and her cousins the piano, while Anu was sent to learn Indian dancing. The boys were all sent to a convent, English-speaking school while she was sent to a school where the medium of instruction was mainly Gujarati.

Later in life, she realised that the regional-language school she attended had taught her some good values in life, though she admits — "but in those days I felt very small." Her English was not up to the mark. "But today, I've realised that my self-worth is not linked to any language."

However, Anu was a good student at school and was also appointed the head girl. She went to St. Xavier's College where she was more interested in a good social life and having a lot of fun.

She did her Bachelor's in Economics and was then admitted to the Tata Institute of Social Sciences to get a post-graduate degree in medical and psychiatric social work.

But throughout her upbringing, the subliminal messages from her parents continued — that all this was good but ultimately she had to marry and have children. "So I got that message and deep down I wanted very much to get married."

Her rebellious nature asserted itself briefly when she acquired a Jewish boyfriend, whom her parents disapproved of, due to his lack of education. Ultimately, Anu went on to marry another Parsi, Rohinton Aga, whom she describes as a 'gem' and who was instrumental in shaping her, more than anyone else did.

"We had a small family business and my brothers were constantly told that they had to look after it. I didn't even know that women could join the family business," says Anu.

In bringing up her own children, Anu was careful not to give conflicting messages to her daughter, Meher and son, Kurush. Both of them were encouraged equally to study, to have a career and to work hard. "I was asked to cook and do so many things which girls had to learn. I've not made her (Meher) do anything. She doesn't even know how to stitch."

It was Anu's father A S Bhathena who had set up the family business — it started out as Wanson India in 1966, the same year that Meher was born, and metamorphosed into Thermax in 1980, when Anu's husband, Rohinton became its Chairman and Managing Director. He was a product of Cambridge and Harvard Business School.

The first of the unhappy incidents in Anu's life occurred a couple of years later in 1982, when Rohinton suffered a heart attack to be followed by a paralytic stroke, which left him with a condition called aphasia, that impaired his ability to speak and also affected his memory. It took him nearly two years of concentrated efforts and will power to undo the debilitating effects of the stroke and restore him to his former brilliance.

Rohinton Aga was a workaholic and thought that Anu was wasting her time at home and prodded and encouraged her to join Thermax. Reluctant at first, Anu joined the company in the Human Resources (HR) department in 1985. This proved to be a fortuitous move, as later on when she had to take on the job of running the company, she found that her biggest advantage was that she knew all the people there.

In 1991, Anu took charge of the HR functions in Thermax.

The '80s and the early '90s were a busy period for Thermax, which was growing by leaps and bounds. It was no longer just a boiler making company. In 1987, it collaborated with Japan's Sanyo to introduce vapour absorption machines. A couple of years later, it formed a joint venture Thermax Babcock & Wilcox, and in 1992, it formed the power generating division.

In February 1995, Rohinton took the company public, with an issue of six million shares, which was oversubscribed seven times.

Their pleasant family life came to an end in 1996. Rohinton had a second and fatal heart attack on February 16, 1996. It threw the family out of gear. On the one hand, it was a personal loss for Anu (she doesn't like to call it a tragedy and refers to it as an event) who had considered Rohinton as the mainstay of her life. On the other hand, he had left behind him a vibrant and growing company of which she was the majority shareholder, and as such she felt responsible for it.

The company's board met and the management approached her to take over the company and run it. For Anu, it was a difficult decision. She knew the company — so far as its people went — but she had no idea about the manufacturing side of it nor was she familiar with its financial position.

But she decided that for the sake of the employees, she would take over the company. She couldn't let them down. The company was anyway being run by competent professionals who knew their job well and she was confident that she could rely on them for help and advice.

On February 19, Anu was appointed as the Executive Chairperson and her daughter, Meher became a Director.

"When I took over the helm at Thermax, I knew a lot about the people in the company. I had not bothered to learn about technology or finance. But I did not feel bad about asking people to explain things to me. I was sufficiently intelligent to understand things if they were explained."

"I was determined that as the head, I owed it to my company to see that it was looked after. So I listened to people," says Anu. She adds, "And I think I can make good decisions."

Fate, however, wasn't done with her yet. Within a year, she had to deal with another painful death — that of her 23-year-old son, Kurush, who died in a car crash.

Both mother and daughter turned to Vipassana, a Buddhist system of meditation, as a way to deal with these personal losses.

In an interview to Accenture's in-house magazine, Vaahini, several years later, Aga said of that phase in her life, "It (Vipassana) helped me to discover my inner strength and centredness. Daily practice has helped me to come to terms with the deaths that I experienced, and in a way, has prepared me for what I had to face on personal and professional fronts."

"Life has taught me that we cannot control our external circumstances (such as an event like death) but we can decide how we will respond to these events, and that decision will shape our lives."

"I have realised all of us can be extraordinary but we choose to define ourselves as ordinary, because then we can be indulgent and not demand the best from ourselves. When we have accomplished our goals and feel bloated, we need to remind ourselves that we are quite ordinary. This attempt to balance keeps my ego in place and pushes me towards meaningful action."

"I have learnt to make time for people who matter, and to invest in meaningful relationships, so that I am not consumed with guilt when the person is no more."

Already close, the unfortunate incidents brought the mother and daughter duo even closer as they became dependent on each other to share and alleviate their unhappiness.

Running Thermax

There was a life to live and a company to be run. In a speech she made some years later, to a gathering of business leaders, Anu said, "I realised I had a choice — either to feel helpless and wallow in self pity, allowing my sense of inadequacy to grow, or to hold myself together and take charge of my life."

She also realised that if she wanted to project Thermax as a successful company, she had to project that sense of success within herself — not as a pitiable victim of circumstances, but as someone who rode the tumultuous waves of misfortune until she reached calmer waters.

"In retrospect, I can see that a CEO becomes a leader when she is able to lead her own life with a sense of well being, before she attempts to lead others. Life will keep on presenting hurdles and challenges, it is an important attribute of the leader to face the world with equanimity. One needs to find one's own centre — a calm and still zone within."

And so Anu took charge of her life. And of Thermax.

The year that she took over the company, Thermax bagged the biggest order it had got until then, testifying to the faith that its customers reposed in it, despite the fact that they had lost their dynamic leader.

In 1998, Anu decided that since the company was anyway being run by very able professionals, it was only right that she should move on to a non-executive role and allow them to take the executive decisions.

"I pretended to run the company for two years," she says self-deprecatingly. "But I got fed up of this pretense. I thought, I am not really running it, so let me become non-executive."

In the late '90s, the Indian economy was going through a bad patch, and for two years in succession, there was a downturn in the manufacturing sector. Since Thermax was dependent on order inflows from manufacturing companies for its energy products and services, the slowdown had an effect on the company.

Thermax had also diversified into too many unrelated areas. Anu says that this could have been due to her husband's decision-making ability being marred by the stroke he had in 1982. The company had ventured into sectors such as software, electronic systems and grain silos. Or it could have been that he realised the latent potential in these areas long before anyone else did. "In some areas, my husband's vision was great. We were the first company to get into wind energy, but before the tax breaks were offered. So it wasn't a viable venture then."

There were rumours floating around at the time that the company would be sold. "The thought never entered my mind. We had so many people depending on us, our reputation was at stake. Not once did it strike me — I could have sold it when we were doing well and the shares were up. But not when we were down," says Anu.

Meher says that they were unable to figure out what was happening. "We knew we had to turn the organisation around, and it was beyond us to do it. We thought, we didn't know the art of turning it around. That we would need external help."

So they called in the experts.

This idea — of hiring consultants — was resisted by the senior managers of Thermax. Recalling it later, Anu said, "They argued that our performance was affected by the downturn in the environment and that as soon as the economic situation improved, we would be on the path to success. They also felt that at a time when our profits were low, it would not be prudent to give hefty fees to a consulting firm."

Anu, who was still struggling to come to grips with an uncertain business environment, went along with their reasoning for a while, but then when things failed to improve, she decided to act on her instincts.

Boston Consulting Group, headed by Arun Maira, was engaged to identify the problems that the company was facing and to recommend the right strategies to put it back on its feet.

Some tough decisions had to be taken and Anu took them.

It started with the sacking of the then Managing Director and CEO, Abhay Talwade, and along with him went the entire 13-member board of Thermax. Prakash Kulkarni, the Joint Managing Director was elevated to the position of CEO on July 21, 2000. Anu said, at that time, that the situation could have been avoided if the management had been more vigilant — she saw the entire state of affairs as a failure of the top management.

The projects business, which contributed about 40 percent to Thermax revenues then, had been affected by the slowdown; the power generation unit had been blindly ambitious and bid for some independent power projects which did not materialise and thus hit revenue projections.

The company had to be streamlined. The non-core businesses of the company had to be sold off, the loss-making divisions shut down, and a joint venture with Japan's Fuji was dissolved.

It was a rather messy situation but there was no alternative but to do as the consultants suggested. As part of the clean-up act, the company also had to lighten its balance sheet by writing off debts that had accumulated and were being carried over on its balance sheet for four years.

There was a total overhaul of the business structure with the appointment of heads for each business unit, who would be responsible not only for making profit for their units, but also for the company. For the top management, a large part of their compensation became performance-linked.

Those were stormy months for the company and all these changes were being carried out under the full scrutiny of the media. But the entire exercise paid off. In 2001-02, the company that had made a loss of Rs 13.2 crore the previous year, now made a profit of Rs 28 crore.

In January 2001, the entire board was reconstituted. Boston Consulting had also suggested paring down the workforce as part of the restructuring. In August 2001, Thermax announced a voluntary retirement scheme, which reduced its employee strength by about 400-odd people.

Anu stayed on in her position as the non-executive chairperson till 2004. Meantime, in 2002, Meher had been appointed Vice-Chairperson, and it fell upon her to carry through and complete the restructuring which had been set in motion two years back.

In 2004, Anu made another decision — to totally relinquish control to her daughter and the management, handing over to them the task of running the company. The decision to step down wasn't easy and she had to do a whole lot of soul-searching before she could put her thoughts into action.

Ever since her husband had died in 1996, she had been catapulted into a frontal role — indeed she had become a role model for aspiring corporate women chieftains. After being in the full glare of the public and the media, which lost no time in lionising her when she took over as the boss at Thermax, she wondered whether she would be able to step away from the limelight.

"I did not regret the decision to step down — but it was tough. I had a routine where I was working for most of the day. How would I structure my days now? How would I find a sense of purpose? I attracted a lot of media glare at that time. What if I missed it?"

In the end, she decided that she just had to do it. She just had to let go.

Passing on the Baton
Meher: The Reluctant Successor

Once Anu had made up her mind to quit as Chairperson of Thermax, she was confronted with a problem. Meher, who was the natural successor to her position, was not as ready to take it on, as Anu had been to give it up. Her daughter had her own insecurities which she was battling with.

She had tough acts to follow — her father, the dynamic Rohinton, whose presence still loomed large over the company and at least in the lives of the two women, in terms of the legacy he had left behind; and her mother, Anu, whose reputation had assumed almost legendary proportion, especially after she had successfully stemmed the slide in the fortunes of the company, bringing Thermax out of the morass it was in and restoring it to its former glory.

Anu told her daughter straight out that she had anyway decided to step down and that Meher had no choice other than to take up the reins. It took a year and a few sessions with a mentor, before her daughter could muster up the required courage.

But once Meher had made up her mind, she threw herself into the role and job.

Meher, the older of Anu's two children, was born in 1966, the same year that Wanson India was set up. Her earliest memories are of going to visit the company's factory in Chinchwad when she was about five or six years old.

She grew up virtually breathing and living Thermax. Her parents' conversations were centred around the company, which they were busy nurturing at the time, and their home saw a constant stream of visitors from the company.

Meher and Kurush were brought up in a liberal atmosphere — with both Anu and Rohinton being careful to maintain equality between the children. Meher always had this idea at the back of her mind that she would have a career of her own, though she did not think in terms of joining Thermax.

"At one point I remember, I wanted to have a chain of coffee shops. I had very entrepreneurial ideas and dreamt of doing something on my own." At one point, she had considered studying psychology and even medicine. Like her mother, she was also remarkably unambitious. "I did not have that driving ambition to be the best, to climb the corporate ladder or to be a high-flying corporate executive."

Her parents allowed the children to pursue their passions and do what they wanted to do. "Both of them were very encouraging. We were told — 'Do what you want to do, but do it well and have passion in what you do.'"

Rohinton was the typical protective father and by the time Meher was 22 or thereabouts, he was prepared to get her married. His stroke had also made him a little insecure, which was manifest when Meher was out with boyfriends, especially those who were not Parsi. Though liberal in most other respects, he was very particular that Meher should marry someone from their own community.

As a student, Meher was good at Mathematics but she was not fond of reading and literature. Her one major accomplishment was on the piano. She was so talented on the piano that it was generally thought that she would be a virtuoso.

But Meher was rebellious, a trait she inherited from her mother. She loved the piano but hated being made an exhibition of.

"I didn't want to do it. I liked it (playing the piano) but I didn't like being made to sit there and it being imposed on me. I used to hate it when people came over and I was made to play. I hated all that. It was so embarrassing."

Anu hated it even more when her daughter was playing and anyone among the audience started talking. She wanted everyone to listen to her daughter in silence. Today, it's been a while since Meher has played the piano, though Anu constantly urges her to take it up again.

Meher had an affinity for the sciences and eventually took up Chemical Engineering, which she enjoyed a lot. She obtained a post-graduate degree in the subject from the Imperial College of Science & Technology in London, and joined Thermax in 1990, as a trainee engineer.

She joined the company in its water-treatment unit, working alongside a few hundred other trainees who had joined along with her. Shortly thereafter, she married Pheroze Pudumjee and both of them together were sent to the United Kingdom, to manage a small, ailing Thermax subsidiary there.

When her father Rohinton died, Meher was in England with her infant son and could not immediately get away and return to India, as she had to arrange for her son's passport and that took a while. After she returned to India, she was appointed a Director in Thermax, in 1996.

Still vulnerable from the tragedy of losing her father, Meher got a further jolt when her younger brother, Kurush, lost his life in the car accident.

Meher recalls that at the time, she had felt angry and unfairly targeted by the Gods. "Dad had already suffered a heart attack earlier, so we were kind of prepared for any eventuality of that kind. But my brother — I really felt God was horrible."

The women turned to each other for emotional support.

When Anu turned 61 and announced her retirement at a press conference, it shocked Meher, as that was the first time she was hearing about it. It also upset her. Unlike Anu, who did things on impulse — who describes herself as very reactive and given to taking decisions on the spur of the moment and thinking of the consequences later — Meher took time to think over her decisions, mull over them, weigh the consequences and then decide on the course of action. Anu's sudden decision left Meher unprepared, since she hadn't really thought in terms of running the company.

However, with Anu sticking fast to her decision, Meher had

no choice other than to acquiesce, though it took her nearly a year to make up her mind. In an interview she said, "The biggest challenge for me was to overcome the doubts I had about my credibility, to feel comfortable with myself and most of all, to be true to myself."

A big lesson in leadership that she learned from her mother was that she was different from her parents, and as such, it was perfectly legitimate for her to make her own mistakes and develop her own leadership style.

As Executive Chairperson, Meher lost no time in fast forwarding the growth of the company. In 2006, the company posted a record profit of Rs 123 crores, up 77 percent from a year earlier. The company won awards for designing innovative heat absorption chillers.

A year earlier, Meher had been named among India's Top 30 achievers by *India Today*, while the next year she won a Young Achiever award from the *Financial Express*, the first of several such accolades to come her way.

Expansion of the company, in the first few years after she took over, was rapid. Thermax extended its reach across South-East Asia, Africa, Europe, the Middle East, China, and North America — all the while adhering to the high standards of ethics and social responsibility that was a hallmark of the founders.

"To us, respect and reputation matter a lot. The kind of business we are in — we do a lot in fire-coal and fire-oil but we do a lot of things in bio-mass too. We do a lot on waste heat. My father had envisioned the company in terms of — 'if we are going to pollute, then we had better clean up.'"

"The vision for our company is to be a globally respected organisation — which means not just numbers. It's much more than numbers."

In the years since she's taken over, Thermax's total revenues have risen more than four times and profits have grown close to six times. For the year 2010-11, the company declared a dividend of 450 percent, up from the 50 percent it had announced in 2002.

Thermax was one of the few companies which weathered the economic downturn rather well — it stood strong in the face of the global financial crisis which plunged the world into a recession in mid-2008 and early 2009. Though revenues saw a dip for two years, the company bounced back in 2011, with a 60 percent rise in revenues and 7 percent rise in net profit.

Meher admits to having been obsessed with work earlier on in her career, especially when she was in an executive role. But now that she has moved to a non-executive role, she says she is finding time to do more things.

Her children, of course, remain her priority, along with a sense of social responsibility and commitment to green technologies. She describes her fight for social causes as being driven by pragmatic considerations of spreading equity, in contrast to her mother Anu, who takes on individual causes with a missionary zeal and crusading spirit.

"I wouldn't describe myself as really working for the underdog."

Music is a great passion with her, a legacy from her father Rohinton, who loved Western classical music, and from her mother's side of the family, who were aficionados of Hindustani classical music. As a child, music was a constant presence around her, with musicians being regularly hosted by her parents while she would often fall asleep to the soothing strains of Bach and Beethoven played on her father's gramophone.

Despite being adept at the piano, she never could summon for the instrument the enthusiasm that she displayed for choral singing, which she discovered after she joined the college choir in London's Imperial College. It has stayed with her ever since.

Every Tuesday, Meher makes it a habit to join Pune's Chamber Singers choir, where she sings second soprano — where she is not a mother, not a daughter, not the Executive Chairperson of Thermax, but just another voice raised in homage to the sublime masterpieces of Western classical greats.

In an interview to the newspaper *Mint* in 2008, she said, "We are a group united by a common passion — the love of singing. It's my getaway to a different place. It's something I do for myself, not for anybody else."

The business successes that both women have seen notwith-standing, their overriding passion and concern still lies in doing something for society and its people — it remains the overwhelming theme in their existence and work.

Within Thermax itself, there are various programmes designed to make it a more inclusive place to work, inculcating a partici-pative culture. There are open forums held periodically, where employees, especially women, can voice their concerns and griev-ances, and Meher, in her usual methodical fashion, takes the time to go through them to try and find solutions.

As Anu later explained — "We belonged to a totally middle-class family. I rarely had a few hundred or a thousand rupees with me when I was young. Now I have a lot of money and am manag-ing crores of rupees. But to me all this wealth means that I can do what I want for the people."

10

THE ACCIDENTAL ENTREPRENEUR

Kiran Mazumdar-Shaw

CEO
Biocon India

Kiran Mazumdar-Shaw, the Founder and boss at Biocon India Ltd, is often held up as the poster-girl of Indian women entrepreneurship, her journey in getting to where she is today, having become almost the stuff of legends.

The humble beginnings of her company in her garage, the way she battled prejudices against women entrepreneurs when she tried to get funds, the skepticism she met with, coming from various quarters, and how she overcame all these hardships, to become the top bio-pharma company in the country — have all become part of business folklore in the male-dominated sphere of corporate India.

Having gained eminence in her field and the credibility that comes with it, Kiran has now transferred her attention to larger issues, such as bringing some coherence into the drug industry, especially from the regulatory perspective, and highlighting the undue advantage being given to multinational pharma companies, who are obstacles in the way to providing affordable healthcare in India.

Kiran, however, was not always the confident lady, leading from the front, that we see today.

As a child, she did not show any hint of the leadership or trailblazer qualities that came to characterise her in later life. She was a quiet, diligent girl, good at her studies, with nothing remarkable about her. She was more of a follower than a leader.

One of her teachers, Anne Warrier, said of her later, "Kiran was a good, obedient, diligent student who did very well at studies. But I would never have thought she had it in her to be so independent, confident and so entrepreneurial."

Kiran's father was the Managing Director and Head Brewer at United Breweries in Bangalore, and the three children — Kiran has two younger brothers — led a 'charmed life'.

"I had a happy childhood and we grew up in a very protected environment. I owe my secure bent of mind to that happy childhood."

Kiran studied at Bishop Cotton Girls' School, and after her schooling, she wanted to pursue medicine, but was unable to get admission to any of the medical institutes because she did not have the required marks. She went to her father and demanded that he pay the capitation fees so that she could study medicine. Her father refused.

It was a big disappointment for Kiran who then joined Bangalore University, from where she graduated in Zoology, with a top rank.

She got a call from London University for a doctorate pro-gramme in genetics, but academics did not interest her, nor did she want to do conventional things. Her father then suggested that she should look at brewing as a prospective career.

"There are very few, good, professional brewers in the country and there is a shortage of talent. Why don't you try it?"

Kiran was aghast. She and a brewer? Why, she did not even like beer. Her antipathy to alcohol was such, conditioned by social taboos against those associated with the liquor industry, that she was often ashamed to reveal at school and college and to her friends, that her father was a brewer by profession.

"How can I be a brewer? What kind of a job is that for a woman?"

Her father replied that it was a perfectly respectable job and brewing was a science, and as such, not to be scoffed at. Having learnt it in Scotland, he wrote to Ballarat University in Australia, which offered a brewing program.

It normally took in people with some experience, but thanks to her excellent grades in college and with the backing of her father, she was accepted at the institute for the programme.

Kiran was in Australia for only a couple of years but it was a life changing episode for her. It transformed her from a diffident girl to a confident woman. That entire experience of living alone in a strange land, far removed from the safety and comfort of her family, having to fend for herself, and being the only woman in a male-dominated career programme, brought out hidden reserves of courage in her.

"I blossomed there and developed a lot of self-esteem, which was lacking when I was in India."

The journey by air from Bangalore to Melbourne was the start of her lesson in self-confidence and self-reliance. She was offloaded from the connecting flight from Singapore as it was overbooked, and had to fight to be accommodated in another flight.

Gregarious by nature, she formed lasting friendships in those two years. She was also virtually adopted by an Australian couple there, who took her under their wing and made sure she enjoyed her stay in that country –something that she looks back on with fond and vivid memories.

"I was like a part of the family. They took me everywhere. Every other weekend, they would pick me up and I would spend the day with them. Every time they went to Melbourne, they would take me along to see a show or something."

The Australia stint also taught Kiran that she could hold her own amidst the cross-culture of students who had enrolled there to learn the art of brewing. All the other students there were men, since brewing was still considered a male domain. They also had previous experience of some kind in brewing, yet Kiran managed to outperform them.

This gave her added confidence in her abilities. "I could grasp things very fast and I could come up to speed with them, despite my lack of experience in the business. And I felt that I was smarter than them."

Two years later, she was a certified Master Brewer and came back to India brimming with confidence, ready to join the brewing sector. But she had still to run the gauntlet of the Indian industry where brewing was not a mainstream profession and women brewers were practically unheard of.

Immediately on her return, luck was on her side. Her father had become a consultant and had been asked to commission a brewery — Jupiter Breweries — in Calcutta (now Kolkata).

Kiran's father put her on the job where she could use her newly acquired skills. She stayed in Calcutta for a year, with Vijay Mallya and his mother. She successfully commissioned the brewery, in the process, teaching Vijay a few tricks of the trade.

"I took a lot of pride in playing such a hands-on role in commissioning the brewery."

Kiran however was not keen to stay and work in Calcutta, and after the job with Jupiter was completed, she approached Vijay's father and the promoter of United Breweries, Vittal Mallya, for a job in any of his breweries in Bangalore or Delhi.

To her consternation and amazement, he turned her down — because she was a woman. He told her that though she held the requisite qualifications and he knew that she was competent enough to do the job, it was a moot point whether, as a woman, she would find acceptance with the male workers in the breweries and with the unions.

"It would be difficult to give you a job. It's a man's work."

Kiran argued that she had managed to deal successfully with the unions in Calcutta and had found no problems working with the men there. Vijay also spoke up in her favour, extolling her expertise and efficiency, but the senior Mallya remained obdurate in his stand.

That was the first time Kiran had come across any gender prejudice and she realised that many occupations may be closed to women — simply on account of their being women.

Her further experiences in her quest for a job as a brewer only reinforced this fact. Women were not wanted in the brewing industry. She did quite a bit of troubleshooting for a number of breweries but when it came to employment, they had no place for her.

"That's when the hard fact hit me. There is a gender bias... or rather a gender challenge. How do I get people to accept me as a woman brewer?"

It was disheartening. After a while, she decided to give it up and instead, look for something outside India. Kiran was one of those rare women for whom marriage, husband and children were not the sole aim. She had to have a career.

She did get a job offer from Scotland but before that happened, she met Les Auchincloss from enzyme-maker Biocon Biochemicals of Ireland, and he asked her to help him start a subsidiary in India, supplying brewers, packaged food companies and fruit-juice makers.

Kiran agreed and for a while, she worked as a trainee manager in Ireland, learning the fundamentals of enzyme-manufacturing. Once back in India, she set up Biocon in 1978, as a biotechnology company manufacturing industrial enzymes which were used in the brewing industry.

"I did not do any market research for enzymes in India. I just jumped into it. All I knew was that the enzymes they were making had some application in brewing and were made by a fermentation process. That connection was there, a link with what I had learned."

Enzyme technology was a new area and Kiran was excited by the prospect that she could help the brewing industry in India and bring some sophistication to their methods of making beer.

She started off the venture in the garage of their house in Bangalore, with around Rs 10,000 as the initial capital, while a 3,000-square-foot shed nearby served as her factory. Her very first employee was a car mechanic.

It wasn't easy. She knew the science of it but needed the funds.

And it was difficult to obtain funds from anyone. In the late '70s, India was in a state of transition and unrest. The emergency imposed by Indira Gandhi in 1975 was lifted in March 1977, and the Congress Party was booted out of power as an angry electorate voted for change and brought in the Janata Party and its rag-a-tag coalition partners — the first non-Congress government of Independent India.

The basic needs of the population were not being met. The government under the Janata Party was largely interested in witch hunting, and its single point agenda was to nail Indira Gandhi for the alleged 'excesses' committed by her government during the emergency period. There was little or no appreciation of enterprise and entrepreneurial talent, least of all that shown by a woman peddling an unknown technology.

Biotechnology was virtually unheard of in India at that time and banks had no inclination to be adventurous to advance funds for a venture which they knew nothing about, and that too, one run by a young woman with no known credentials.

Requests for money were either flatly refused or they asked her father to stand guarantor for her, not willing to listen to her plea that as Managing Director of the company, she would be the guarantor.

Kiran says that though things looked difficult at that time, she never thought of quitting. In fact, all the opposition she met with only made her more determined than ever that she should forge on and prove them all wrong. The bias against her gender especially firmed her resolve to soldier on.

"At that time, I was in a strange mood. I never wanted to give up and I rose to the challenge. I was determined to succeed. I felt that I had got to prove these people wrong — people who still had old-fashioned notions as to what a woman could or could not do."

Everywhere she went, she was told she was a bad risk.

She does, however, admit that she once told her Irish partner that maybe he should look for some other business partner in India, as nobody seemed to believe in her idea, especially given that she had no business experience. She even introduced him to a businessman in Delhi for that purpose.

He, however, told her that he wanted to partner specifically with her, as his company wanted someone with her talents and qualifications. "He had more faith in my abilities than I did," says Kiran. He encouraged her to persevere.

At a friend's wedding reception, she vented her grievances to someone who was a General Manager with Canara Bank. The next day she was pleasantly surprised when the bank called her up to say that her loan had been sanctioned.

That was a beginning. Getting funds was just one part of it. Her business was expanding and she was rapidly outgrowing her garage. She had to find space to set up a manufacturing facility and she also needed people. She was facing intense resistance in both areas.

There were very few people with the kind of technical skills that her company needed at that time. Even if they had the skills, people were unwilling to join a start-up biotechnology firm with a woman at the helm of affairs. Things were further compounded by the appalling lack of infrastructure needed to run a successful venture — uninterrupted power supply, sterile laboratories, and high quality water among others.

Kiran kept going with dogged persistence, the support of her father and her stubborn conviction in her business being her main solace and support.

In the beginning, she was just making enzymes for the brewing industry and others. The scaling up was rapid. Within a year of starting the company, Kiran began exporting enzymes to the United States and Europe, and Biocon became the first Indian company to accomplish this feat.

A little over a decade after coming into existence, Biocon had firmly established itself as a market leader in the biotechnology field and recognition came fast, as it was India's first such company. Help also came from unexpected quarters such as Narayanan Vaghul, former chairman of ICICI, who helped her with funds when she wanted to upgrade her technology.

He was impressed with her passion, her dedication to her venture and her deep commitment to biotechnology. In an interview last year, with a business magazine, Kiran said, "When I wanted to scale up our technology, I could not find anyone in India. There was no venture funding. No bank wanted to touch it. Nobody wanted to fund a home-grown technology launched by some young scientist." But Vaghul told her that these were exactly the kinds of new technologies that ICICI was looking to fund in the country.

Kiran counts Vaghul as one of her mentors in the industry. "There were people who believed in me. I suddenly realised it's about being able to articulate and share your concept in an articulate way with somebody and get people to buy into what you are saying. If you can do that, then you are sure to succeed."

Kiran says that she always wanted to do something different and out-of-the-ordinary and not just follow conventions and norms. "I've also been driven by a sense of differentiation. I didn't want to be a 'me-too'. I wanted to do something and be someone different."

"Leadership is about influencing change. I know what it is like because I had to influence change. Since I was a victim of that resistance to change, I wanted to influence it all the more. As a woman leader, I want all women to have the kind of respect and opportunity that I struggled to get in my earlier days."

A confident woman can open any door if she is determined enough. At the time that Kiran was setting up her business, it was the height of the 'license raj' in India. Nothing could be done without greasing palms or knowing the right people.

Kiran was told that it would be practically impossible for her to get the required permissions at Udyog Bhavan in Delhi. Despite the warning, she was able to get a senior bureaucrat, Mr. Biswas, to help her with the formalities in acquiring the licenses necessary for her venture.

"He bought into my story and went out of his way to help me. He gave me the permissions, licenses, everything I needed — without having to pay a single bribe." She, of course, also told Biswas that every time she visited him and was waiting to see him, she was approached by certain 'fix-its' offering to speed up her paperwork for a monetary consideration.

Within the first three years of setting up her business, Kiran knew that biotech was going to be a game-changing venture and by 1983, she had set up a facility to commence research.

In 1989, Biocon became the first Indian biotech company to get funding from the US for proprietary technologies. In 1990, Biocon's in-house research program was upgraded, based on a proprietary, solid substrate fermentation technology. That year, she set up Biocon Biopharmaceuticals Private Limited to make a select range of biotherapeutics in a joint venture with the Cuban Centre of Molecular Immunology.

Biocon was doing very well but Kiran was not satisfied. She wanted to expand beyond enzymes now and wanted to get into the biopharmaceutical space. "Enzymes are very self-limiting. The market for them was small and the opportunities few. I was not able to grow very fast."

In 1994, she set up Syngene International as a subsidiary of Biocon, to undertake custom research for the pharma sector. A couple of years later, in 1996, Biocon made its debut in the bio-pharmaceuticals segment with the manufacture of statins. Bio-pharmaceuticals refers to medical drugs produced using biotech-nology. Statins are a class of drugs used to lower cholesterol levels.

In 2000, the company entered the area of specialty pharmaceu-ticals, setting up a fully automated, submerged fermentation plant for that purpose, and Kiran floated a second subsidiary Clinigene, to pursue clinical research and development.

Indian pharma companies are primarily makers of generic products — that is licensed copycats of drugs which have been researched, developed and patented by others, mostly multina-tional drug firms. So there was no need for clinical research.

Clinigene was India's first clinical research organisation.

Biocon was in a high growth phase. It now needed massive funds to sustain that growth rate as well as to finance its expan-sion of the plant manufacturing statins and its foray into human recombinant insulin.

In 2004, Kiran took the company public and it created a history of sorts. The company raised Rs 315 crore with an issue of 10 crore shares, and the initial public offering was oversubscribed 33 times. It was the first issue by a biotechnology company in India. On the day it listed, it closed on the exchanges with a market capitalisation of more than a billion dollars.

The product that Kiran started out with — enzymes — was no longer core to Biocon's operations; by now it had rapidly transformed into a full-fledged biopharma firm. In 2007, it was decided that the company would focus exclusively on pharmaceuticals and healthcare. Kiran sold off the enzymes division to Novozymes for $115 million.

In 2010, she struck a $350 million deal with the world's largest drugmaker Pfizer, to sell the Indian company's insulin products globally. In March this year, the alliance was called off, the US company saying that it would develop its own insulin drug.

"When we did the deal with Pfizer it was a big thing, because after all, it is the world's largest company. And I also did very well financially on that deal. But I am a realist. At the back of my mind, I knew that Pfizer could change its priorities someday in the future."

"The split didn't really change anything for me, because until 2016, I was not expecting anything big from Pfizer. Biocon's job was to develop the programmes and hand over the baton to them and they would take it into the market globally."

"I will still go ahead with the programmes for which Pfizer gave me the money. What changes for me is that instead of giving the programmes to Pfizer, now I will have to give it to multiple partners."

Kiran points out that in emerging economies like India and in the rest of Asia, regional companies have stronger marketing clout compared to big multinationals.

She doesn't rule out another tie-up with Pfizer, if needed, for another set of products. "For this particular portfolio, it didn't work out. It's not the end of tie-ups."

Focus on Insulin, Cancer and Affordable Healthcare

"I am in pursuit of newer things, so I want to see what I can do to improve disease outcome."

Insulin is a crucial drug for treating diabetes and assumes life-saving proportions, especially in the case of Type I diabetes, where patients have to inject themselves with insulin doses, and most people are scared of taking injections.

"If you administer insulin early on, it has a much better effect, so that's why we are developing oral insulin."

Her oral insulin failed to clear clinical trials last year and Kiran intends to do more research on it, before moving on to the next phase. But she remains confident of the market opportunity and the need for such a product.

Biocon is also producing anti-bodies, for both cancer and auto-immune diseases. Cancer cure is very close to her heart, especially since her husband John Shaw — whom she married late in life, when she was 44 years old — was diagnosed with kidney cancer in 2009. Luckily, the cancer was detected in the early stages and prompt treatment sent the tumour into remission.

"A cure for cancer is a huge unmet need. We are not able to address most types of cancers, and there are many types of cancers for which we have no solutions. I feel so helpless.

"I am not just looking at prolonging a person's life by a few weeks or months with anti-cancer therapies. I am looking at a more long-term cure for cancer. Instead of cancer care, I'm looking at cancer cure."

Affordable healthcare is top on Kiran's agenda, particularly, availability of drugs at lower costs. Biocon has a range of branded formulations covering diabetes, cancer, kidney diseases, cardiology and auto-immune diseases. She plans to double the size of her offerings from the current Rs 250-odd crore to Rs 500 crore in the next two years. The total size of the branded drugs market is estimated to reach $55 billion by 2020.

"I am very concerned about affordable healthcare. I feel people (read multinational pharma companies) are besotted with getting governments to pay anything... just because they've developed a drug, they think they can charge whatever they want. Most pharmaceutical companies are not troubled by this moral dilemma."

Kiran has been fairly outspoken about what she sees as multinational drug firms ruining the name of the entire pharmaceutical industry.

It was necessary for big pharma companies to have a dual strategy for the developed world and the emerging markets, as the latter were becoming an important market for these companies. "They can have different strategies, especially with regard to pricing, and to be more sensitive to the needs of countries like India."

The pharma industry and the regulators were not in sync with each other, with the regulators making it a difficult environment to operate in and the drug makers looking for protection.

"The question I ask is — why is it that in every other industry, there is a varied choice of products, while in the pharmaceutical industry, we don't have the same choice?"

She cites the example of the automobile sector where a consumer has the choice of buying a luxurious Mercedes or an economical, efficient Maruti car, even though all cars serve the basic purpose of conveying us from one point to another.

"The same way in pharma, why can't we have 10 different types of products at varying prices, with customers having a choice in what to buy?"

The doctors and the pharma firms were in a conspiracy to convince customers that one particular product was better and safer than another. After all, all drugs are released into the market for sales only after extensive trials and once they are certified as safe.

"I'll give you an example. Look at statins. Now if you want to reduce cholesterol, you can take a simvastatin, a pravastatin, an atorvastatin or rosuvastatin. If you look at the way all these drugs bring down cholesterol, they are all the same."

"Why shouldn't I, as a patient, have the choice of what to take, rather than the doctor prescribing it for me? Today, drug companies have brainwashed us into thinking this (a particular medicine) is a super Rolls Royce drug, while actually it may be nothing of the kind."

Patented drugs have become expensive because the regulatory environment ensures that a company would have to spend at least a billion dollars in research before it can be released in the market.

According to Kiran, regulators have become unnecessarily paranoid and stringent about lengthy clinical trial for drugs, which makes the whole process time-consuming and expensive.

"Safety should anyway be a post-marketing concern, which is how it is today."

She is also a strong votary against compulsory licensing which she feels may strangle innovation and research.

The Trade-Related Intellectual Property Rights (TRIPS) agreement allows governments to issue a compulsory license allowing someone else to produce a patented product or process without the consent of the patent owner to address public health concerns.

The licence, however, can be issued only three years after a patent has been granted and the producer needs to pay a royalty to the patent holder, at rates fixed by the government. The first instance of compulsory licensing was seen this year when Natco Pharma was allowed to launch a generic version of Bayer's kidney and liver cancer drug, Nevavar.

"I am totally against compulsory licensing."

Kiran has very clearly defined growth verticals which will take Biocon forward, into its next phase of evolution. The small molecules business, the biosimilar insulin vertical (biosimilars are products which are marketed after the expiry of patents on existing biopharma products and which have the same properties), the biosimilar mAbs (monoclonal antibodies) vertical, the branded formulations vertical that is largely India-centric now but which Biocon wants to take global, novel programmes (licensing and partnering of assets) and the research services business.

"If you look at all these, I think we are clearly focused on how we want to see ourselves in the future. We want to be known as a very strong, insulin-led, diabetes company. Diabetes is a very important therapy for us. We see ourselves as being very important in chronic therapies like the ones we are developing because these are life-long therapies. They are very expensive. If we can make them affordable, we can make a huge impact on healthcare. That's how we have looked at our mission."

Biocon is now a Rs 2,000-odd crore company with a market cap just slightly below the $1 billion mark. In the next 10 years, Kiran sees the company that she has nurtured and built becoming a global player. "Right now, we are already making a global impact but we are known globally as a high quality, biopharmaceutical company. We are threatening a lot of big players."

"To be a real global player, I think it'll take us at least 10 years to make our presence felt."

Biocon is already a significant player in emerging markets and for the company to be a global player it has to increase its presence in the developed economies, especially the US, where the value is much higher.

Kiran has come a long way professionally but on a personal level, it is still her family with whom she relaxes over the weekend. Her niece, nephews, her brothers, her 81-year-old mother and her two dogs are whom she wants to be with, as she unwinds from being a super-entrepreneur to just being Kiran.

●

11

I SHALL OVERCOME...

Kalpana Saroj

Chairperson
Kamani Tubes

The young woman took a revolver out of her handbag and laid it on the table in front of her. She looked at the man sitting on the opposite side — the man who wanted to end her life — and spoke to him. "I don't know you. You don't know me. We are strangers to each other, not related in any way. I have not harmed you."

She paused.

"Why then, do you want to kill me?"

It was a small police station in Kalyan, a suburb in Mumbai, India's financial capital, where people came to live their dreams. The policemen watched the scene with interest.

She indicated the revolver in front of her. "There are six bullets in this. You can try and kill me — you can do it now, but I know how to use this. I am not one of those women who will sit passively and allow you to do whatever you want; I can defend myself."

The man folded his hands in supplication. "Tai, forgive me. I did not know who you were. Please forgive me and let me go."

The young woman's attempts to purchase a piece of land in Kalyan had attracted the attention of the local land mafia and the criminal elements in the area. The owner of the land wanted to raise money to get his daughter married and had been looking to sell it, but the land was mired in so many litigations and court cases, with an obstinate tenant refusing to vacate, that nobody wanted to have anything to do with it.

When he approached Kalpana, the young woman, to help him out, she saw it as an opportunity to get into the real estate business. She already had a small, flourishing furniture business but she wanted to diversify into something a bit more lucrative like real estate. She knew that the land was under dispute, but she had very little knowledge of how the real estate sector worked. She did not even have any idea of the importance of clear title deeds or what it would take to get the property transferred to her name. All she had was her network of contacts, and a strong conviction that she could leverage those contacts, to make that piece of land hers.

"I can do it," she told herself. "I can get it done."

She did not have the required money with her, but she took a small bank loan and bought the disputed land for Rs 2.5 lakh.

Then she set about the onerous task of settling the various disputes and litigation. It took her a while, and she was helped along the way by a series of happy coincidences. She tenaciously followed the progress of the property file as it made its way from one government office to another — incredibly, the Assistant Collector who signed the necessary papers to release the property from Kul-Kayda,* became the Deputy Collector by the time the file again reached him, for his sanction to free it from the Land Ceiling Act. When she wanted the final approval to make over the title deed in her name, she found that the Collector had gone on leave and the Deputy Collector was officiating for him. To her, it seemed like the Gods were conspiring to make the impossible happen.

By the time she was eventually done with clearing the land of all the legal complications, its market value had gone up to Rs 50 lakh. It was at this time that her transaction began to get noticed by the local goons and land sharks who thought that she — a woman, an interloper from a remote hamlet in Maharashtra, belonging to a community considered to be outside the pale of society — should not aspire to this kind of success and should be eliminated. It was to be a contract killing, carrying a price tag of Rs 5 lakh.

Kalpana heard about the heinous plot against her through a man who knew the goons involved, but was sympathetic towards her. He warned her that there were people out there who were envious of her success — the land that she had bought was seen as a virtually useless piece of real estate, since nobody had been able to free it from the morass of cases it lay enmeshed in — and who wanted to get her bumped off.

"Go back to your village," the young man advised Kalpana. "It's not safe for you to live here any longer."

"Go back?" asked Kalpana. "I have nothing to go back to. There's nothing in my village for me anymore. This is my life and

---

*In the pre-Independence era, most of the arable land was owned by a few, rich, landlord families. Several Kuls (families of labourers) used to take care of the agricultural activities of their landlords, for generations. Landlords weren't directly involved in day-to-day work, but would appropriate a big part of the income generated from the farms. As a result, social status and economical conditions of the labourers' families wouldn't improve, and there was no chance of it getting better in the near future either. Kul-Kayda (labour family law) forced those landlords to distribute ownership of their lands among hard working labourer families.

I have to stay here. No, I won't be frightened by these people. If I could deal with everything else that has happened so far, I can deal with them too."

Death itself held no terrors for this woman who had seen and experienced death at close quarters. She refused to succumb to threats to her life because she had to fight for the sake of her family who depended on her for their survival. She could not let them down.

Thanking the man for the warning and assuring him that she could take care of herself, she procured a fire-arm license for herself and bought a revolver. After all, her father had been a policeman and she knew about guns.

Then she went to the police commissioner there and told him, "What kind of laws do you have, when a young woman tries to do some honest work and do a good turn to someone, there are people who openly threaten to kill her? What kind of protection are you providing to women like me?"

The commissioner was amazed at her accusation and got the local police station to look into her complaint. Kalpana had ferreted out the names of the men who were planning to assassinate her.

It did not take the police long, to search and arrest the band of men whose enmity she had incurred.

"Kalpana had the satisfaction of seeing her would-be killers punished and brought to book. She had done it, as she had promised herself. With the land now in her name, she brought in a Sindhi partner, a land developer, to jointly construct residential and commercial buildings on the land she had acquired. She grandiosely named it Kohinoor Plaza."

"Kalpana's career as a real-estate developer was launched under the banner of Kalpana Saroj & Associates."

The Child Bride

Mahatma Gandhi called them Harijans or the Children of God. They are the former untouchables of the caste-ridden society of India, where discrimination on the basis of caste is legally forbidden, though in several parts of the country, demarcations on the basis of class and caste are still rampant, giving rise to feuds and atrocities.

They are now denoted as Dalits. The word, which has its origins in Sanksrit, means 'ground', 'suppressed', 'crushed' or 'broken to pieces'. Dalits are found all over India but they do not form a homogenous class in terms of common ethnicity or religious heritage. What they do have in common is their crushing poverty, attributable to the class and caste distinctions which had their beginnings in social divisions during Vedic times, and which degenerated into a racist segregation to enable certain members of the social hierarchy to subjugate others. About 90 percent of the poor in India are Dalits.

When Gandhiji called them Harijans, it was meant to empower them and liberate them from the caste-based discriminatory practices against them. However, the Left parties and missionaries advocated the use of the term Dalits as more appropriate, and the name has stuck ever since.

Bhimrao Ramji Ambedkar or Baba Saheb Ambedkar, the father of the Indian Constitution, is the pan-India icon for Dalits, having fought for their rights and upliftment.

It was in this community that Kalpana Madhao was born, in Ruparkheda, a remote little village in Maharashtra's Akola district — consisting of a few straggling houses, one dirt road running down the middle and some paddy fields nearby. Hers was a mid-sized family consisting of three boys and three girls, of whom Kalpana was the oldest.

Her grandfather had been a worker in a farm, barely able to feed his family, but he managed to educate one of his sons, Kalpana's father, until the seventh standard. This enabled the young man to get a job as a policeman. His own education — limited though it was — motivated him to educate his children as well.

Kalpana was a naughty and high-spirited girl, but clever, with an aptitude for studies. She often played hookey from class, playing pranks and stealing guavas from the trees with her friends, but these misdemeanours were overlooked by her teachers who saw the spark of intelligence in her.

Destiny, tradition and mindsets were against her. Education was not a priority in her community, and even if her father was in favour of getting his children, and especially his girls, educated, the family was not similarly predisposed. She was a girl and she had to get married as soon as possible. Her mother had been married at 9 and it was natural that her daughters should be married at around the same age. Kalpana's father did manage to stall her marriage as long as he could, but at the age of 12, one of her uncles brought information about a suitable groom.

"Enough," he told Kalpana's father. "It's high time she got married. She's already 12 and she should be looking after a household of her own now." Her father gave in to the pressure.

Kalpana was reluctant. She cried. She remonstrated. But the weight of her circumstances was too much for her lone voice to protest against. She could not shake off the centuries of conditioning that dictated that it was the lot of a girl to get married and look after her husband's family. Her mother had ensured that she was suitably equipped with all the skills of a homemaker — cooking, cleaning and caring.

The dreams of the child-bride were shattered even before they could take shape. Her family had only the vaguest idea of what the groom did. He and his family lived in one of Mumbai's slums — in a shanty that was little more than a room. Into this was crammed Kalpana and her husband, his parents, his brother and his wife and their seven children.

Her husband worked as a helper somewhere, his brother worked in a harmonium repair shop and her sister-in-law was a domestic help elsewhere. So the burden of running the entire household fell on the shoulders of this 12-year-old child.

Kalpana would be up early — at 4 in the morning. She had to have a bath before embarking on her household duties — to clear the dirty vessels, clean the house, and cook for the entire family.

And for all her troubles, all she got was abuse and beatings — especially from her brother-in-law and his wife. Any shortcomings in the food (too much salt, too little salt, overcooked or undercooked) or in the cleaning of the house were greeted with the choicest abuses and physical assault.

She cooked for everyone in the house, but often went hungry herself, as she was denied food as punishment for her perceived failures.

Within a short time she was a changed girl — the laughing, happy, spirited girl was replaced by a malnourished, frightened being with lank, unkempt hair falling all over her face. Her father, who came to Mumbai on work at the police headquarters, about six months into her marriage, couldn't recognise his little girl when he went to see her.

He was aghast. This was not why he had married off his daughter. He resolved to take her away from there. Her in-laws initially protested and vowed not to give her up, but could not do anything against his authority as a policeman.

Kalpana returned to Ruparkheda and her marriage was dissolved. Her father told her to forget everything and continue her education. Getting back to the village rescued Kalpana from the cruel life in Mumbai but exposed her to an entirely different set of problems.

As a woman with a failed marriage, her status changed and fingers were pointed at her as if she were in the wrong. Veiled and not-so veiled barbs and insults were levelled against her every day. In the eyes of the villagers, she was to blame for not having had a successful marriage. Even her own mother and her family members treated her with contempt and disdain. It was as if a stranger had come to live in their midst. She was almost like a pariah and an outcast.

At this time, Kalpana was in an emotionally fragile state. Her experiences as a bride had cowed her spirit and the aftermath at the hands of the villagers, served to lower her further in her own estimation. She thought that working and earning money would solve her problems — at least it would make her financially independent.

Her first thought was to get into the police force. They had just started recruiting women from her village. When she went to speak to the person in charge of the police station there, he sympathised with her situation but told her that she would have to wait till she was 18, before she could join them. "I suggest that you complete your matriculation and then come back."

Next, she thought of taking up nursing as a profession but again, she was declared under-aged. Her third option of joining the military also came to naught. Desperation was now setting in for Kalpana. Her marriage had been a disaster from the start, but she had got over it. Now her efforts to fend for herself and gain financial independence were being met with uniform resistance. She decided that she had to acquire some skills and she learned how to sew and how to operate a sewing machine.

Kalpana's father was unaware of the mental trauma that his daughter was going through. It was not the kind of household where children could talk uninhibitedly to their fathers and confide in them. He was a strict, authoritarian figure who had to be obeyed and respected.

Things came to a head when someone said something particularly nasty about her. It broke Kalpana's already fragile spirit and she began to contemplate suicide as the way out of all her troubles.

Her life was a total failure every way she saw it and she seemed doomed — there was nothing to live for anymore, she felt.

She went to the local chemist's shop to buy Tick 20 — a poison used in killing bed bugs. She bought three large bottles, to ensure that the quantity would be sufficient to kill her at once. She spent the rest of that day meeting some of her close friends, as a farewell gesture. Her house was too crowded for her to carry out her ghoulish deed in peace, so she went down to her aunt's place, about a kilometre or more from her house. She told her aunt — who lived alone — that she wanted to spend the night with her. The aunt was more than delighted to have her niece stay with her.

Towards evening, Kalpana told her aunt, "I'm feeling sleepy. I'll go in and lie down for a while."

As soon as she was alone in the bedroom, Kalpana quickly opened the bottles and drank the contents straight off, anxious to get the job over and done with. She got into bed and pulled the covers over her head. She imagined that the poison would take effect when she was asleep and she would die peacefully in her sleep.

The poison had tasted vile. Its effects were worse. In a short time, her body went into spasms and she started foaming at the mouth. Her aunt, who came in with tea at that moment, was frightened to see her niece thrashing in agony. She quickly called for help and Kalpana was rushed to the local hospital in the village.

The doctor in attendance was pessimistic about her chances of survival. He said that he would try to cleanse her stomach but it would be 24 hours before they could give any kind of verdict. It was touch and go.

24 hours later, Kalpana was still alive.

I Will Survive

That close brush with death brought about a critical change in

Kalpana's attitude, especially when villagers and those close to her began to say that if she had died, people would have indeed confirmed their notions that she was at fault for her situation. They would have said that Madhao's daughter had committed suicide to hide some awful misdeed she had committed.

"I decided then, that now on I would live, and do something significant in life. I would show everybody that I can survive and can make something of my life. Now, I would no longer think of dying."

Once she had recovered, she realised that staying on in the village was impossible. She had to find work and that was possible only in Mumbai, the nearest city and the land of opportunities. When she broached the idea with her parents — both of whom had been devastated by her suicide attempt — they were doubtful. How could they send her daughter all alone to the city again?

But they were a little apprehensive about saying 'no' to her, in her state of what they considered an 'unstable' mind. Her father approached one of his brothers, who stayed on Bapat Road in Mumbai and made a living selling fried *papads*. He was reluctant to host her because he stayed alone in a slum and he was not sure if he could answer for the safety of the girl when he went off to work.

Empathizing with her plight however, he spoke to a Gujarati customer of his, a train driver who stayed in the railway quarters below the bridge, near Dadar station. Her uncle explained the situation to him and asked him if he would allow his niece to stay with them as 'as one of their daughters.'

The Gujarati man and his wife were kind people and they took her in. This exposed them to a lot of slander and vicious rumours among their neighbours, but they ignored it. He got her a job in a hosiery unit in a textile mill compound nearby.

Kalpana's first day on the job started off on a bad note. Brought up in extremely conservative surroundings, where speaking to boys was taboo, she was dismayed when she saw men and women working together in the hosiery unit.

She had learned to operate a sewing machine in her village, but fright and the strange surroundings combined to make it difficult for her to work the machine that was in the factory. It refused to co-operate with her.

"So you've been lying, have you? You don't know how to operate the machine," asked one of the supervisors impatiently, after watching her ineffectual attempts to work on it. "Now you better get out of here and stop wasting our time."

Kalpana was in tears, her dreams of earning a living vanishing before her eyes. One of the other supervisors took pity on her and put her to work cutting the threads which were used for stitching. It was the lowliest job available and it fetched her 2 rupees a day.

For Kalpana though, it was big money — money she had earned through her efforts, and as such to be prized. Within a month, she also got over her hesitation and learned to operate the sewing machine. This immediately upgraded her status to a bona fide seamstress and her wages went up to Rs 215 a month.

"That was the first time I saw a 100-rupee note and I was thrilled."

Little more than a child, Kalpana's life during those days was one of unceasing toil. She lived from day to day, learning the hard facts of life in a brutal way. Learning to live in a huge, crowded city like Mumbai was in itself a task. She did not know how the trains operated or how to read the indicators.

One day, she took a train intending to go to Dadar but ended up in Churchgate instead, and was nearly trampled by the hordes of women who were in a hurry to get out of the train. A kindly woman watching her distress took her aside and gave her a brief lesson on how to navigate the suburban train network.

In the meanwhile, her father lost his police job, and as the eldest child, the responsibility of looking after the family devolved on her.

She rented a house in Ulhasnagar, near Kalyan, and brought her family to stay with her. Those were tough times for the family, and for Kalpana in particular. One brother and one sister died due to lack of timely medical help and no money.

"My sister died, pleading for her life… She wanted to live. She didn't want to die. I was helpless, I could do nothing. I was shattered."

She now had to augment her income. She took a job in the Sun Mills compound in Sewri. She would leave for work at 6:30 in the morning. She worked all day, then returned home to do some more tailoring work on a couple of sewing machines she had installed in her house.

Her poor origins, her privations and her struggle to maintain a livelihood put her on the path to undertaking activities that would alleviate the misfortunes of others. She founded an organisation to provide employment and livelihood to people who were educated but unemployed.

Her outfit spread awareness among the unemployed, educated segment that there were government schemes that could help them set up their own businesses and ventures. She was herself without any significant, formal education, but she helped others get loans from banks.

Emboldened by the success of those whom she was helping, she herself took a loan and started out on her first venture — a furniture shop. She married again, but her husband died in 1989, leaving her with two small children.

All along, Kalpana's thoughts were centred on providing sustenance for herself and her family. Her goals were limited. It was during this time that she slowly built her base of contacts — the police, bureaucrats and local politicians — and she toughened herself to cultivate an attitude whereby she could approach anybody to voice her grievances and to get things done.

"My contacts are my best capital."

The Troubleshooter

Her first foray into real estate had nearly cost her her life. It was only her presence of mind, and her fearless tackling of the situation, that had saved her.

She had been successful in her first attempt to neutralise her enemies. But that didn't stop the intimidating tactics that her opponents and detractors adopted to thwart her in her attempts to establish herself in the property business.

In her next venture, Kalpana found herself up against the local corporation and government functionaries. When she wanted to start work on a building, the officials showed her the development plans that included a provision for a public road which would run through the middle of her plot. She pointed out that there already were substantial roads on either side of the plot which would serve the purpose and there was no necessity for a road right in the middle of her land.

"It was being done deliberately, since they could not stomach the idea of a Dalit woman being successful in the real estate sector."

When the corporators remained obdurate in their stand, Kalpana did not stop to argue more with them but went straight to Gopinath Munde, who was the Deputy Chief Minister of Maharashtra at the time.

She told him, "I am a Dalit woman. In pictures, in the media, there are things said about encouraging backward women to come forward and work. In your speeches, you talk of progress. But when a woman like me tries to do something, there are people trying to obstruct us."

She then explained her problem to him. "If anybody can make me understand why this road needs to be built in the middle of my plot, I will stop all construction work. But I have to be convinced about it."

Munde called the Municipal Commissioner and asked him for an explanation. He then stayed all land development plans in the Kalyan-Dombivli belt. "That was a big decision."

The municipal commissioner asked her why she had gone with her problem to the Deputy CM. "You could have spoken to us directly."

Kalpana asked him in turn, "But do you listen to me? I have been trying to talk to you all to make you understand, but so far it has fallen on deaf ears."

Her issue was resolved and she was allowed to go ahead with her plans.

The harassment did not stop there. Each success of hers fanned the ire of her opponents, who disliked the idea of an interloper prospering in an area which they considered as their fiefdom.

She had another plot of land which she had acquired from a landowner belonging to the Thakur community. A compatriot needled him, "This unknown Dalit woman is going to construct such a big building here? What will it do to our reputation as men?"

Kalpana was slightly apprehensive about taking on these men, since they were related to local Congress leader Kripashankar Singh and he could easily wield his clout to get the police to torture her and get her to back off from the land. However, she knew all the policemen in the area and had gained their respect through her charitable work.

The Thakurs filed a few court cases against her to make her stop her work and they even had her assaulted by hoodlums armed with choppers (a weapon that is a cross between a scimitar and a machete). Kalpana finally had to resort to writing to Sonia Gandhi, explaining to her about her work and telling her that her own party General Secretary was harassing her. Sonia removed the erring functionary from his post and wrote to the then Maharashtra Governor, advising him to take action against the party leader.

The Governor sent a message to Kalpana, telling her that she needed to file a complaint with the state Home Secretary to initiate action.

Kalpana, however, decided not to pursue the matter, since her own affairs had been settled to her satisfaction. "It was not my intention to trouble others. But I won't tolerate people who try to take away my rights or interfere in my legitimate work. If they do that, I'll fight back."

Her reputation as a troubleshooter grew by word of mouth. People realised that here was a woman who could get things done, who was in a position to influence events and people.

Kalpana's journey to success was grim, tortuous and full of strife. It was no easy path that she had to tread. While with each success, she gained confidence in her ability to do things and get things done, it also increased the number of her antagonists and those who could not tolerate her success. But it only intensified her determination to do better.

Her successes fuelled her ambition. While previously, her only wish had been to live a comfortable life, she now realised that she had it in her to go further than that. She could do a lot. She had survived.

Kamani Tubes: Saviour to the Rescue

Kamani Tubes, a part of the Kamani Group of Industries presided over by well-known industrialist Ramjibhai Kamani, was set up in 1960, and had been a leading manufacturer of non-ferrous alloys and tubes used in industries such as power generation, air conditioning and refrigeration, petrochemicals and sugar.

It had been a very profitable company and had, at one time, produced 60 percent of the nation's requirements. In the mid-

1970s it got into financial trouble because of a crisis within the Kamani family. Feuds between the family members and lack of attention to the companies within the group saw the empire disintegrating.

In the '80s, its condition worsened, and between February and April 1981, it was closed down since the banks refused to lend more money unless their outstanding loans were cleared. It was re-opened when the State Government intervened and a temporary settlement was worked out.

In October 1983, the management declared a lockout over an incident involving the Chief Executive and a few workers. The factory re-opened in Feb 1984, but the situation did not improve. The management said that it had no resources to run the company. By the end of that year, workers were not getting their salaries. They appealed to the banks and to the State Government to take over the company but there was no response.

Then in February 1985, the factory shut down altogether, because electricity and water supply connections were cut off over non-payment of dues.

Various solutions were tried out over the years but nothing worked. Neither were the Kamanis interested in running the factory nor would they allow anyone else to take it over and run it.

In 1988, a workers' co-operative society took over the company after the sanction of a rehabilitation scheme by the Board for Industrial and Financial Reconstruction. It was hailed as a landmark move at that time and was cited as the first instance of a successful initiative run by workers.

But the workers ran into problems trying to implement the revival scheme and the factory again sputtered to a stop in 1995, and subsequent attempts to revive the company remained nonstarters.

Its operating agency, Industrial Development Bank of India (IDBI), invited interested parties to take over the assets of the company — which consisted of a couple of heritage buildings in Ballard Estate, filled with tenants who were paying low rents and refusing to vacate, a rented factory in Kurla and four acres of land in Bangalore.

All of it fetched barely Rs 3.5 crore. The company had 500-odd workers and two unions who did not see eye to eye. Nobody was willing to take on the company as it looked too troublesome to be turned around. It had run up debts of Rs 116 crore and there were about 140-odd cases against it being fought out in various courts. Apart from the dues to creditors and banks, Kamani Tubes had not paid workers' salaries for years, including their statutory dues, all of which ran to more than Rs 8 crore.

The position was such that in the year 2000, a section of its employees who stayed in the Kalyan-Dombivli area came to her asking for her help. Some had taken to begging at the bus stands for their survival. They had a pathetic tale to narrate. Their children were turning to crime to fulfill their basic needs.

Kalpana remembered her own poverty-stricken childhood and what her family had gone through, and she was moved by the plight of these workers and their families.

"Nobody was willing to take on the responsibility of reviving the company. But I did and there was a reason for it. The workers who came to me told me that at one time they used to get 100 percent bonus. And now some of them were dying of starvation, illnesses and poverty."

"It struck a chord in me since I myself came from a poor background."

She decided that she was in a position to help the workers. She had nothing to prove and nothing to lose. If she could do something for the company and the workers, it would be a feather in her cap while she would get the mental and moral satisfaction that her life had been worth something. If she failed, well, at least she would have the satisfaction of knowing that she had tried.

Thus Kalpana reasoned with herself.

She got to work in her usual fashion — working her contacts. This was a bigger job than anything she had tackled until then and she required support — influential support — as well as funds. Friends and people whose opinions she sought on the matter told her that she was crazy to even think about it.

She approached a friend of hers, who had political affiliations, whom she viewed as an older brother, for his support. He told her that she was attempting something that would probably ruin her, but since it was something close to her heart and was in the interests of the workers, he would extend her every possible assistance.

Next was another close friend who stayed in London, who was involved in philanthropic activities for his home state, Gujarat. She told him, "Why don't you utilise some of your money for reviving this company. If the company turns around, I'll pay you back when it starts making profits. If it fails, think of it as money that you donated for a good cause." He agreed.

She leveraged all the goodwill she had accumulated over the years. She borrowed money from wherever she could. She staked her all on this project. She sold off Kohinoor Plaza, her first venture in the real estate sector.

Kalpana first formed a committee consisting of experts in their respective areas, such as manufacture of non-ferrous tubes, marketing, finance, administration and so on. Together, they drew up a comprehensive revival plan for the company with details about how to repay debts, how to re-start the factory and run it, first raising funds and then expanding the expenditure plan.

This plan was submitted to the operating agency IDBI which took it to the court. It took six years for the scheme to be approved by the courts.

It was not a simple matter. Her troubles had just begun.

The creditors were happy with her scheme and were supporting her. But there were three obstacles which she had to overcome to put her plans into action.

The Ballard Estate property was on Mumbai Port Trust land and they wanted their dues of Rs 1.06 crore to be cleared before they supported her scheme.

Kalpana approached the Mumbai Port Trust chairperson at the time, Rani Jadhav, and presented her with a post-dated cheque, assuring her that once the scheme was cleared by the court, she would get her dues.

"I have incurred a lot of debt because I have borrowed heavily to get this company running. If you do not accept this post-dated cheque and we do not get your support for this scheme, I will soon have to join the list of unsecured creditors who throng the courts every day. I'm trying to do something for the workers and their families. You have to help me."

Mumbai Port, a central government undertaking with very well-defined and rigid rules and regulations, did not, as a rule, take post-dated cheques, but Kalpana's earnestness and her conviction carried the day and the Chairperson accepted it.

In Kurla, Harsh Goenka of RPG Enterprises who had taken over Kamani Engineering, had been refusing to support the scheme until Kamani Tubes vacated the factory premises which it had rented. She gave the Goenkas an undertaking in the court, that she would get the place vacated once her scheme was cleared, and she got that support too.

That left the unions — or at least one of the factions that was inimical to her plans. This was a segment of the union that had tried to run the company earlier and failed. It comprised about 10 percent of the workforce. Kalpana had promised to give the workers all their arrears, amounting to about Rs 5 crore, and they had initially agreed to it. But when they saw her smoothing out all the litigation and saw how its value was being unlocked, they grew greedy and demanded a bigger amount than what had been agreed upon.

Kalpana had appointed a battery of lawyers to settle the court cases; she had cleared the tenants in the Ballard Estate building and had got the creditors and all other parties over to her side. The court had also appointed her the President of the company in the year 2000, to oversee the day-to-day functioning of the company.

In 2006, her scheme was formally approved and she was given time till 2001, to turn it around and make it profitable. She was also made the Chairperson. The union tried to block her scheme in court, but the court overruled it saying that since they had failed to get the company back on track once before, they had no locus standi to object to the plan — which was now the sole chance of revival for the company.

She was given three years to pay off the workers' salaries — she did it in three months and at one go, and gave them an extra Rs 90 lakh, as a goodwill gesture. She also paid Navinbhai Kamani, the former Chairman, his dues of Rs 51 lakh, as part of the restructuring exercise of the company.

During the years that the court cases were being settled, she was also doling out Rs 500 every month to each of the workers, that was the most she could manage. But at least it ensured their survival.

Her next milestone was to nurse the company back to health. The court-mandated deadline was 2011. Last year, the company was brought out of SICA (Sick Industrial Undertaking Act) and from the purview of the Board for Industrial and Financial Reconstruction, after it made a profit of Rs 5 crore.

"I am proud of what I have done and what I have achieved. This was a company which had nothing — it was absolutely zero. Now it is worth at the very least, about Rs 500 crore. During those days, I used to think that if I am not able to revive it, just maybe, I would have had to again contemplate suicide. That is because I had taken on so much debt, committed myself to so many people

— it was a huge responsibility. I couldn't have stood failure. I had gambled everything in my life on this one venture.

"Sometimes when I look back, I am myself amazed that I managed to do it... and I ask myself - did I really do it?!

"My goal is to take Kamani Tubes back to its former days of glory when it had a global reputation and its products used to be sold far and wide."

Kalpana had the factory shifted from Kurla to Wada in the Thane industrial zone, which was inaugurated about three years ago, with an investment of about Rs 300 crore.

The company currently has revenues of around Rs 40 crore. There are plans to take the company public in the near future, but only once it has started making stable profits. The Kamani brand has been revived in the Gulf region through Al Kamani International in Kuwait, and Kalpana Saroj LLC in Dubai, to cater to the demand for copper tubes in that region.

The plan is to get into the manufacturing of copper alloys, so that its range of activities would span mining, smelting and the finished products. Kamani will also soon start exporting its products to the Gulf regions and Europe.

Apart from Kamani Tubes, Kalpana also has interests in real estate, sugar, steel and mining.

She has plans to convert the Ballard estate building into a luxury, boutique hotel. In 2007, Hollywood actor Tom Cruise had approached her with a proposal to take over the building and build a hotel there. However, the deal did not go through as the price he offered was too low.

Kalpana still works 16 to 18 hours a day. It has only been hard work that has brought her all her success in life. "Work is worship for me. I wouldn't know what to do without work. When I started working with Kamani Tubes, I would often wish there were more hours in the day so that I could work longer."

Kalpana's philosophy in life is that if you work hard and with honesty, the entire universe will conspire to help you in your endeavours.

Not having had much time to spend with her children and family in earlier years, she now takes time off (although it is still rare) to go shopping or to watch a movie with them. She likes to cook for her family and whenever she gets the time, she enjoys tending to the plants in her garden.

She has a son, who is a pilot with Air India, and a daughter, who is in the hospitality industry. Her third husband helps her in the running of Kamani Tubes, while her son-in-law, Ashish Deshpande, is the Chief Executive Officer of the company.

Her former life, especially her first marriage is now a distant nightmare for her. The sister-in-law, who used to torture her, approaches Kalpana frequently for help and assistance. And in fact, Kalpana has helped her, for instance, by giving her money for her daughter's marriage.

"I am not vindictive by nature. I take things positively. I always think that if I had not been treated badly by them, maybe I would not have been what I am today. It is not in my nature to dwell too much on negative things. I'm content to let bygones be bygones."

Kalpana's story reads like a fairy tale with all the ingredients of a rags-to-riches fable — but the fabric of the fairy tale has been woven, not with magic wands, fairy godmothers or bottled genies, but with hard grit, determination and unremitting toil against extreme adversity.

●

ACKNOWLEDGEMENTS

I wish to acknowledge and express my gratitude to those who have been major influences in my life.

My parents who brought me into this world — To my father who taught us to be fearless and hard-working, and forbade us from using the word "can't" with respect to doing anything, right from threading a needle, riding a bike, climbing a mountain to whatever caught our fancy; for inculcating the habit of reading in us, giving us the freedom to experiment and expand the boundaries of our minds beyond the immediate narrow confines of our physical world.

And to my mother who, widowed at a young age with four children on her hands, took on the mantle of being the bread-winner without any prior preparation or experience, and ensured that we educated ourselves as much as we wanted while she displayed an unexpected acumen for financial planning and financial investments for always being there for me, for making sure I ate my meals properly.

I want to thank my siblings — two brothers and a sister — who, just by virtue of being elder to me, saw to it that my life was a constant challenge, as I was always trying to keep up with them (and sometimes surpass them) in everything they did, both intellectually and physically.

I want to thank my cousin Ganapathy Aiyar and his wife, who kindly consented to host me in their house in Delhi where I needed to conduct some interviews for the book. They did this at a moment's notice even though Aiyar had last seen me as a 10 year old.

I would like to say thanks to all the people I have worked with through the years, in *Financial Express, Business Standard,* Press Trust of India, the Times group, and Thomson Reuters for giving me all those opportunities, for believing in my abilities and for the measure of recognition that I got as a reporter.

I wish to thank my publishers at Jaico Publishing House for giving me this wonderful opportunity to write the book, especially Commissioning Editor Poornima Swaminathan, who displayed an unusual tolerance in accepting all the changes I suggested while writing the book.

There is a special thanks I need to say to my erstwhile colleague and long-time friend, Dev Chatterjee. He knows what it is for.

I must express my gratitude to all the women who have been featured in this book, for so promptly accepting my invitation to interview them despite their busy schedules. I have to thank them for taking the time out to patiently answer my questions, without any fuss.

And finally, although they will not be reading this, I want to acknowledge my deepest sense of obligation to all the animals I was privileged to keep over the years — dogs, cats and monkeys — they have taught me the valuable lesson of giving and accepting love unconditionally. And how it makes life simpler.